Talking
Tea

Casual Tea Drinker to Tea Connoisseur

ALSO BY JUDITH A. LEAVITT

Talking Tea with the 3Gs:
The First 10 Years of the
Three Generations Book Club (2015)

Talking Tea

Casual Tea Drinker to Tea Connoisseur

Judith A. Leavitt

TalkingTea

In this book, all information regarding health and wellness is provided purely for informational purposes and should not be considered medical advice. This book is not intended to be used as the basis for treatment of medical problems or other health issues. All matters pertaining to your physical or mental health should be supervised by a physician or other health-care professional.

Resource for health claims: *Tea and Health: An Overview of Research on the Potential Health Benefits of Tea*, www.teausa.com

Published in Coralville, Iowa, by TalkingTea LLC

TalkingTea LLC titles may be purchased in bulk for educational, business or sales promotional use. For ordering information, please visit: www.Talking-Tea.com

Manufactured in the United States of America
ISBN# 978-1-735080-90-1
10 9 8 7 6 5 4 3

Cover:
Design by Pixelstudio
Photo by belchonock
Blue teapot by Danny Smythe
Leaf logo by Aleksandra Sabelskaia

Interior: Black teapot by Nadejda Tchijova

Dedication

To Mom

...for my first taste of tea

Contents

Welcome

The Periodic Table of TalkingTea

Part Six – Specific Types of Teas

Resources

About the Author

Drink your tea slowly and reverently,
as if it is the axis on which the whole earth revolves –
slowly, evenly, without rushing toward the future.
– Thich Nhat Hanh, Vietnamese Buddhist monk

Welcome!

I'm so glad you came for a visit. Please sit down and let me offer you a cup of tea. Which kind would you like? Do you have some favorite teas?

Here—take a look inside my tea box. Maybe that will help you choose a great tea.

What's the matter? Are you a bit overwhelmed by all of the options? I stock only the 48 most special teas, so surely you can select one that matches your mood and your personal taste. I'm guessing it's not easy for you to pick a tea from my huge collection. But let me help you change that.

Starting today, I invite you to begin a journey of tea exploration. In the chapters of this book, you will discover amazing things that will increase your enjoyment of every cup of tea you drink. You will also become far more confident about trying new teas and sharing your favorite ones with your friends.

Through this fun and educational book, you'll become more knowledgeable about all types of teas, including many specialty and premium teas not sold in grocery stores. You'll also become one of an increasing number of individuals who move from casual tea drinker to tea connoisseur!

As Henrietta Lovell writes in her delightful book, *Infused: Adventures in Tea,* "I hope to seduce you, a little, into a love of loose leaves."

PERIODIC TABLE of

TalkingTea™

Talking-Tea.com

WHITE
160-170°F
Steep 2-3 minutes

YELLOW
170-180°F
Steep 2-5 minutes

GREEN
170-180°F
Steep 2-3 minutes

OOLONG
180-200°F
Steep 3-5 minutes

BLACK
190-205°F
Steep 3-5 minutes

PU-ERH
200-212°F
Steep 2-5 minutes

COUNTRY OF ORIGIN —

C : CHINA   **I** : INDIA   **J** : JAPAN   **S** : SRI LANKA   **T** : TAIWAN

WHITE:
- Bai Hao Yin Zhen — *Silver Needle* (C)
- Bai Mu Dan — *White Peony* (C)
- Shou Mei — *Long Life Eyebrow* (C)
- Gong Mei — *Tribute Eyebrow* (C)

YELLOW:
- Jun Shan Yin Zhen — *Silver Needle* (C)
- Huo Shan Huang Ya — *Yellow Sprout* (C)
- Meng Ding Huang Ya — *Yellow Sprout* (C)
- Mo Gan Huang Ya — *Yellow Buds* (C)

GREEN:
- Bi Luo Chun — *Green Snail Spring* (C)
- Long Jing — *Dragonwell* (C)
- Anji Bai Cha (C)
- Mao Jian — *Downy Tip or Hair Point* (C)
- Huang Shan Mao Feng (C)
- Tai Ping Hou Kui — *Monkey King* (C)
- Chun Mee or Zhen Mei — *Precious Eyebrows* (C)
- Tianmu Shan — *Qing Ding* (C)
- Xin Yang Mao Jian — *Fur Tip* (C)
- Lu An Gua Pian — *Melon Seed* (C)
- Hyson — *Lucky Dragon* (C)
- Pan Long Yin Hao — *Coiled Dragon* (C)
- Zhu Cha — *Gunpowder* (C)
- Houjicha (J)
- Bancha (J)
- Sencha (J)
- Genmaicha (J)
- Kukicha — *Twig Tea* (J)
- Matcha (J)
- Gyokuro — *Precious Dew* (J)

OOLONG:
- Feng Huang Dan Cong — *Phoenix Mountain* (C)
- Ti Kwan Yin — *Iron Goddess of Mercy* (C)
- Wu Yi Shan — *Rock Tea* (C)
- Shui Xian — *Water Sprite* (C)
- Bai Hao — *White Tip or Oriental Beauty* (T)
- Formosa Oolong (T)
- Tung Ting or Dong Ding (T)
- Baozhong or Pouchong (T)
- Qing Xin — *Green Heart* (T)

BLACK:
- Panyang Gong Fu — *Golden Monkey* (C)
- Keemun (Qimen) (C)
- Juiqu Wuling — *Black Dragon* (C)
- Lapsang Souchong (C)
- Yunnan (C)
- Ceylon (S)
- Darjeeling (I)
- Assam (I)
- Nilgiri (I)

PU-ERH:
- Sheng — *Uncooked or Raw* (C)
- Shou — *Cooked or Ripe* (C)

The Periodic Table
of TalkingTea

According to legend, in the year 2737 BCE, Chinese Emperor Shen Nung accidentally discovered tea. Considered the father of Chinese agriculture, Emperor Shen Nung figured out that it was healthier to boil water before drinking it. One day, as he sat under a wild tea tree, a few leaves from the tree fell into his cauldron of boiling water.

When he sipped the brew, he found it tasty and invigorating, and tea was born! Legend has it that during his later research, the Emperor also began to discover tea's medicinal properties.

Although it's an ancient drink, tea is the most widely consumed beverage in the world next to water. You will find some type of tea in almost 80% of all U.S. households. It is the only beverage commonly served hot or iced, anytime, anywhere, for any occasion.

To make it easier to understand the different categories and types of tea, I created my *Periodic Table of TalkingTea*. Found on the facing page, this chart will become an anchor and guide throughout your journey of tea exploration.

You will see that tea categories are listed on the left side, from lightest to darkest of the teas. Within each category, note the large number of specific types of teas included. The table also shows the recommended brewing temperature for making a perfect cup of each type of tea.

In this book, I will refer to this table at intervals, helping to deepen your knowledge and understanding of the vast world of tea.

For a printable, full-color version of the *Periodic Table of TalkingTea*, go to www.Talking-Tea.com.

EXPLORE

An EXPLORE symbol like the one above will appear at the end of each chapter. As you read these sections, I invite you to explore or try something new and different from your usual routine. You might experiment with tasting a new tea, preparing tea in a fresh way, or blending your own tea from several varieties.

You are about to embark on the wonderful world of tea exploration. Have fun on this journey as you become a true connoisseur of tea.

PART ONE

Where It Begins

Thank God for tea! What would the world do without tea?
I am glad that I was not born before tea.
– Sydney Smith (1771-1845)

CHAPTER 1

The Little Blue Teapot

My love for tea started when I was ten years old, and it began with a little blue teapot.

I remember coming home with my family after church on a bitter cold Sunday in eastern Iowa, and eating our traditional noon meal of fried chicken and mashed potatoes. But after we finished our lunch, Mom announced she was tired and needed a rest.

So she bundled us five kids up in sweaters, coats, mittens and boots and sent us outdoors to get some "fresh air."

For the next couple of hours, we played while running around on a well-worn path between the barn and all the farm buildings. As the sun started to set behind the field of cornstalks, we headed back to the white farmhouse, stomped snow from our boots, and went inside our home.

Shivering from the cold, we crowded around the oil-burner stove as we peeled off our heavy layers of clothing. Once we warmed up, the four girls set the table as Mom made a simple supper of soft-boiled farm eggs and white toast.

Then the magic happened.

Mom pulled out a silver tea ball, filled it with fragrant leaves and placed it in a little blue teapot. Then she filled the teapot with boiling water and waited for it to become tea. After a few minutes, she sweetened the tea with sugar, then poured it into special china cups for each of us.

As a ten-year-old, I didn't know the blue teapot was a famous Hall brand, and I had no idea what kind of tea we were drinking. But to this day, I can recall every detail of that moment—the sound of tea being poured from the teapot into the cup, the warmth of the cup in my hands and the coziness of that farmhouse kitchen

I'm sure that childhood memory has contributed a lot to my current love of tea. I can instantly associate tea with good food, a warm room and the comfort and safety I felt as a child surrounded by a loving family.

EXPLORE

When did you first taste tea? What memories and occasions do you associate with drinking tea? Recall a lot of the details such as where you were, who you were with and foods you had along with your tea.

Invite one or two friends to tea some afternoon and share stories about your earliest memories of drinking tea.

*Tea is wealth itself, because there is nothing that
cannot be lost, no problem that will not disappear,
no burden that will not float away,
between the first sip and the last.*

– The Minister of Leaves at The Republic of Tea

CHAPTER 2

Why We Love Tea

Seven ladies sat around a beautifully decorated table in Susan's warm and cozy dining room. In front of the guests, delicate china cups and plates were ready to be filled with hot, fragrant tea and delicious treats.

Carrying a tray of beautiful teapots, Susan entered the room and poured each guest's favorite type of tea. A few minutes later, she returned with colorful serving platters filled with dainty tea sandwiches and homemade scones.

Around the table, smiling, happy faces welcomed the event, and the women praised Susan for making this gathering so special. I joined them in offering accolades to the host of this month's meeting of *Tea Time*.

In my home community in Iowa, we have a wonderful social club for women who are retired or semi-retired. The larger organization offers a variety of interest groups, including Tea Time, which is my absolute favorite one.

Once a month, the leader divides us into groups of six to eight ladies who are assigned to a host's home for tea and visiting. I am always amazed at the quality and depth of the conversations that take place over cups of tea and creative snacks.

The director of Tea Time always provides a question that stimulates conversation and helps us get to know each other. Often the question will include describing something from childhood and something from the present. This encourages us to share details about where we grew up as well as what brought us to our current home in Iowa.

These gatherings have helped me build new friendships with delightful women. But in addition to the food and conversation, tea has become the link that brings us together.

Tea room magic

Sharing tea and delicacies at a hotel or restaurant tea room becomes a magical experience. Perhaps you have visited one of these venues and discovered the delight of being served a wonderful cup of tea alongside a three-tiered stand of tasty sandwiches, scones and sweets.

As you enjoy tea in one of these settings, you might be surprised by how connected you feel to your tea companions. Having a formal tea with friends will often generate stimulating conversations and shared confidences. Even dressing up for these events adds to the fun of this special experience, all centered around a steaming cup of tea.

Tea as a conversation starter

Meeting for tea often results in conversation that goes beyond the typical chat about movies or recipes. When my friend Lorrie and I started getting together every couple of months for lunch and tea, we created our own small book club. Each time we met, we would discuss a book we had recently read, sharing our thoughts and ideas about it. At one of our recent tea lunches, we talked about the delightful and memorable book, *The Agony of the Leaves* by Helen Gustafson.

For many years before her death, Gustafson was the tea buyer at the renowned Chez Panisse restaurant in Berkeley, California. She also served as a tea advisor to many hotels and restaurants. Lorrie and I enjoyed her descriptions of the tea rituals of her childhood in Minnesota as well as details from her interviews with the leaders from London's Thomas Twining Tea company.

We even tried her recipe for "Pepper Toast," which is simply toasted white bread slathered in butter and sprinkled with black pepper. It tasted surprisingly good.

EXPLORE

Consider forming your own Tea Time group. Simply take turns hosting a monthly gathering that includes serving favorite teas along with a few special treats. Provide a discussion question that encourages sharing details about childhood memories or perhaps favorite movies or books. Appreciate the special social time, the quiet conversations and the joy of drinking tea.

There are few hours in life more agreeable than the hour dedicated to the ceremony known as afternoon tea.

– Henry James (1843-1916)
in *The Portrait of a Lady*, published in 1881

CHAPTER 3

Tea in the Afternoon

Once you've experienced a fancy "afternoon tea," you'll understand why tea drinkers love this ritual so much. It's like having a miniature party while never rising from your chair at the table.

In a formal setting such as a restaurant or tea room, you simply relax and allow others to bring you delicious tea and a three-tiered cake stand filled with tiny sandwiches, tender scones, delectable desserts and fancy chocolates.

I have personally enjoyed afternoon tea in many hotels and restaurants where the experience made me feel pampered and totally spoiled. While I always enjoy these times with friends, I have also appreciated solitary afternoon tea with the company of a great book.

Where did it begin?

Legend says that sometime in the 1840s, a duchess who served Queen Victoria invented afternoon tea to solve a common problem. During this time, most people ate a large breakfast, a light luncheon meal at midday, then nothing until a large heavy dinner served late in the evening.

Because there was such a long gap between the light luncheon and the late dinner, the Duchess of Bedford began complaining that she had a "sinking feeling" in the late afternoon. She started calling for tea along with bread and butter sandwiches or light cakes to be brought to her bed chamber in late afternoon.

Once she realized how much better this made her feel, she invited some of her aristocratic friends to join her, and she moved her afternoon tea into the drawing room of her home. Her guests loved this new activity and soon began hosting their own versions of afternoon tea.

Before long, afternoon tea had become a social event. Now the hostesses created elaborate menus that included delicious cakes, small sandwiches, scones with clotted cream and jam, and enticing sweets and pastries. These fancy teas were served at a short, sturdy table with guests sitting on low chairs or sofas. The setting always included fancy linens, beautiful but delicate china and sumptuous tea treats.

High tea

As afternoon tea became more popular, it soon was clear that this was a privileged event for the rich. For workers in newly industrialized Britain, tea time had to wait until after work.

Because the workers needed sustenance after a day of hard labor, the after-work meal always included meat and a pot of strong tea to revive flagging spirits. Served at the kitchen table with high-backed dining chairs, this meal became known as "high tea."

As you continue to become a true tea connoisseur, be sure you refer to fancy midday gatherings as "afternoon tea," not "high tea." Remember that afternoon tea can be a formal affair, as you'll find at elegant hotels, or it can be as casual as a pot of tea and some cookies shared with a friend.

Hosting an afternoon tea

Consider planning and hosting your own afternoon tea party. This event provides a great way to build relationships at the same time you enjoy delicious food and wonderful teas. Your event doesn't have to be fancy, and you don't have to spend hours cleaning house or preparing special foods. Just gather a small group of people who enjoy visiting over a cup of tea and a few snacks.

If you want to make it elaborate, pull out your best china, silver and linens. Offer variety by purchasing a few different types and styles of tea. For the food, you can learn the skill of making homemade scones and tiny sandwiches. Or you can pull out a couple of favorite cookie recipes and keep your menu simple.

One of my favorite times is enjoying a quiet afternoon tea and a treat with my husband. This has become a Sunday afternoon tradition, and during our tea time, we share many thoughts, dreams and memories.

We also developed a custom where once a year, we would invite friends to join us for a whole-day "salon." We selected a topic such as geography, music or literature and asked our friends to prepare a short report on the subject. Then we gathered in the morning and shared our presentations.

After taking a break for lunch, we continued the presentations until late afternoon, when we stopped for afternoon tea. All of us still have many good memories of the discussions shared during the salon day, especially those around the tea table.

EXPLORE

Invite a few friends for an afternoon salon with tea and guided conversation. It's even more fun if you invite friends you know but who don't know each other. Over tea, ask each of them to respond to an unusual question. For example, describe something about yourself that is the same as when you were 18 years old, then tell something that's different at the age you are now.

PART TWO
Secrets to a Great Cup of Tea

Tea is naught but this. First you make the water boil,
then prepare the tea. Then you drink it properly.
That is all you need to know.

– Sen Rikyu (1522-1591)

CHAPTER 4

Brewing and Steeping Tea

A great cup of tea doesn't happen by accident. Instead, it involves good planning, proper supplies and a bit of patience. But for many of you, one of your biggest changes will be to switch from commercial tea bags to using loose leaf tea.

Many tea drinkers have relied on tea bags forever. They are certainly the fastest, most convenient way to make a cup or even a pot of tea. And in the past, you may have found the taste to be just fine.

But as you become a tea connoisseur, you will notice a difference in the taste, aroma and quality of tea made from loose leaf tea compared to traditional tea bags.

There's nothing wrong with using tea bags, and you don't need to eliminate them from your cupboards. But it might help you to know that tea bags typically contain the dust and fannings, or extremely small particles, from broken tea leaves. So tea from these bags won't have the same depth and quality as loose leaf tea.

For tea leaves to extract the most flavor, they need room to absorb water and expand when steeped. Unfortunately, most tea bags constrain the leaves, which prevents them from expanding enough to reach a full flavor and aroma.

When you steep loose tea in a clear glass pot, you can actually see the tea leaves absorb water as they expand and infuse the flavor of the tea. As you experiment with brewing different types of tea, you'll begin to notice the difference in the quality and flavors with using loose tea instead of tea bags.

The invention of tea bags

In 1908, tea merchant Thomas Sullivan began sending tea samples to potential customers using small hand-sewn cloth bags instead of expensive tea tins. As customers brewed tea in these bags, they realized they liked the convenience of pre-measured tea and the ease of removing the steeped leaves from the teapot. They soon asked Sullivan to provide more tea in these bags, and the convenient tea bag was invented!

Today you can find tea packaged in a variety of tea bags including square, pyramid and round shapes. The bags are usually made with light filter paper, but you can also find ones made from food-grade plastic or silk.

Advantages to using tea bags:

- You can brew one cup of tea at a time.
- There's no mess in your teapot or teacup.
- You don't have to dispose of wet tea leaves.
- Tea bags travel easily in your purse or suitcase.
- You can purchase inexpensive tea bags at grocery stores.

Disadvantages to using tea bags:

- Because tea bags are not large enough for loose leaf tea to expand and infuse properly, they contain smaller particles of tea, which are generally of lower quality.
- Tea in tea bags steeps very quickly and can result in a more tannic, astringent brew.
- Stored tea bags lose flavor more quickly than loose leaf tea, so you need to replace them often.

⬧ Loose leaf teas are available in many more varieties than ones packaged in tea bags.

⬧ You can't see the appearance of the leaf in a tea bag before you purchase it.

If you prefer loose leaf tea but want the convenience of bagged tea, or want to create your own tea blends, purchase a supply of empty tea bags that you fill yourself. Or use paper filters or the metal strainer found in some teapots to have the convenience of loose leaf tea without any mess. You will also find many artisan teas are available in single-serving mesh bags that allow room for the leaves to expand.

The recipe for tea

You don't need a lot of fancy equipment for great tea. In the beginning, gather an inexpensive tea kettle for heating the water, a glass or ceramic teapot and a container of good quality loose leaf tea. Eventually, you might want to purchase a variable temperature electric kettle that takes the guesswork out of getting the correct water temperature for specific types of tea. Here are some essentials for making a great cup of tea:

⬧ *Good quality water*

Most tap water contains minerals and oxygen levels that can negatively affect the taste of tea. So ideally, use filtered water or even bottled water. Don't reach for distilled water because that also lacks the oxygen level needed for making good tea.

⬧ *Proper amount of tea leaves*

Teas vary a lot by volume, so measuring by the teaspoonful may not be accurate. I suggest you purchase a small, inexpensive gram scale so you can get accurate measurements of the amount of tea you will be using.

The usual amount of tea leaves is between two and three grams per six-ounce cup, which is the most common size. Of course, mugs can hold anywhere from eight to twelve ounces, so with a larger cup, adjust the amount of tea accordingly.

◊ *Correct water temperature*

Different types of tea do best when the water is heated to specific temperatures. This may seem picky, but if your water is too hot, it can scorch the tea leaves and cause a bitter taste.

Green teas are especially sensitive to the water temperature. If you've tried drinking green tea in the past but didn't like it, perhaps the water used to steep it was too hot. You may want to try green tea again with water that is heated to a more precise temperature.

◊ *Correct steeping time*

How long to steep your tea can vary a lot depending on the type and flavor of tea you are using. You won't harm your tea by not following the recommended steeping time. But for flavors to have proper depth yet softness, try to stay close to the recommended time.

You can use a standard chart for this, but many companies include the recommended water temperature and steeping time on the outside of the tea container.

Here is a chart that shows guidelines for the main classes of tea. Notice they are listed from the lowest temperature to the hottest water.

Type of tea	Water temperature	Steeping time
White tea	160-170°F	2-3 min.
Yellow tea	170-180°F	2-5 min.
Green tea	170-180°F	2-3 min.
Oolong tea	180-200°F	3-5 min.
Black tea	190-205°F	3-5 min.
Pu-erh tea	200-212°F	2-5 min.
Herbals/tisanes	205-212°F	5-7 min.

You may find directions for black tea that say to use boiling water or 212°F for steeping, but experts suggest a slightly lower water temperature, which prevents the tea from tasting bitter.

Summary of the steps for making tea:

- ⋄ Heat filtered water to the correct temperature.
- ⋄ Preheat your teapot and cup by filling them with hot water, then dumping the water out.
- ⋄ Put the correct amount of tea leaves into an empty pot, then slowly pour hot water over your tea.
- ⋄ Set a timer or watch the clock for the ideal steeping time.
- ⋄ Gently pour the steeped tea into your cup or mug. If necessary, use a fine-mesh strainer to keep the tea leaves out of your prepared tea.

Wow, that was easy! Now sip it slowly and notice the taste and aroma of your perfect cup of tea.

EXPLORE

Just for fun, steep the same type of tea at two or three different water temperatures or for varying lengths of time. Try steeping for two minutes, then taste the tea. Next steep the same tea for three or even four minutes, and taste it. How are the flavors of the teas different? Make notes in a tea tasting journal about your preferred steeping temperatures and times for your favorite teas.

A woman is like a tea bag.
You never know how strong she is
until she gets into hot water.

– Eleanor Roosevelt (1884-1962)

CHAPTER 5

Making the Best Cup of Tea

Once you've mastered the art of brewing and steeping your favorite teas, you'll want to protect your precious tea leaves and supplies. This includes following careful guidelines for storing tea as well as taking extra care with the steps as you make your tea.

Start with purchasing the best quality and type of teas you can afford. Then drink your favorite ones regularly, perhaps even daily. Don't try to use up your *old* tea first and save your good quality teas for special occasions. Instead, buy your favorite special teas in small amounts and replenish your tea cupboard often. Consider great quality tea as a special gift that you can enjoy every day.

Take care of your tea leaves

The flavor and taste of loose leaf tea will slowly deteriorate over time. To prevent this as long as possible, be sure to store all of your teas properly. Most tea vendors recommend storing teas in small, airtight tin containers.

Protect your tea from air, light, heat and odors, which can all affect the freshness of your tea leaves. If you like to store tea in a lovely glass container, simply keep it away from bright light or sunlight.

While it might seem tempting to store tea in the refrigerator or freezer, your tea leaves might absorb moisture and odors that will affect the aroma and taste of the tea. Keep in mind that any place with a lot of moisture, such as a cabinet close to your dishwasher, can also decrease the quality of your tea.

In an airtight container, most black teas will keep their freshness for one to two years, while green teas start to lose their flavor at around six months. That doesn't mean you can't still enjoy teas you've had longer than that. Just be sure to store your teas carefully and use them up within a reasonable amount of time. If you have access to tea vendors, plan to replace green, yellow and white teas each year with fresh teas from the seasonal harvest.

Cautions with brewing and steeping tea

To always get the most flavor and aroma from your tea, give the tea leaves plenty of space. Your favorite tea ball infuser may seem handy, but it will inhibit the "agony of the leaves," or the ability of tea leaves to expand fully in hot water.

For a great cup of tea, measure the correct amount of dry tea leaves, then brew them in a glass teapot. This allows hot water to infuse the largest area of the tea leaf and bring out the flavor intensity. It also gives you the pleasure of watching the leaves as they unfurl. When the tea has steeped, you can strain it into your cup or into a second pot for pouring.

Boil tea water only once

If you get ready to make a fresh pot of tea, start over with new filtered water. Reheating water results in a flat taste which is picked up by your tea.

Don't reheat steeped tea

If your tea gets cold, don't reheat what's left in your cup because that will give the tea a flat taste. Instead, prepare fresh hot water and infuse the original tea leaves a second time.

Keeping tea warm

It's fine to keep your tea warm over a tea light or a small candle. But be sure there aren't any tea leaves left in the pot or your tea will slowly keep brewing and eventually become very bitter.

Use a tea cozy

Personally, I love using a soft fabric tea cozy to keep my pot of tea at a good temperature. You can find a wide variety of tea cozies at specialty shops as well as online stores.

Leftover tea

When you have leftover tea, pour it into a glass jar or other glass container and store it in the refrigerator. When you're ready for a refreshing break, pour the tea over ice cubes and enjoy perfect iced tea.

You can also make iced tea from scratch by using a larger proportion of tea leaves to the amount of water. There's even a new trend of brewing iced tea by simply putting the correct amount of tea into a pitcher of cold water and storing it in the refrigerator overnight. With either method, strain the leaves out as you pour the cold tea into a second pitcher or carafe.

Best tea steeping vessels

Here in the U.S., we usually steep our tea in Western-style teapots, but you can use any type of teapot or container.

Ceramic teapots tend to retain heat the longest, but a glass teapot is always nice for showing off herbal teas and blooming or flowering teas. For an elegant tea service, you might choose a porcelain teapot, since most of them are very delicate and refined.

If you want a contemporary and slightly British feel, you might enjoy using a stoneware teapot, which holds the tea at a very consistent temperature. For some Japanese green teas, consider steeping in a gaiwan, which is a small cup with a saucer and lid.

Be sure to follow the tea purveyor's guidelines to make sure the ratio of tea and water matches the size and style of your steeping vessel.

Adding milk to your tea

Many people prefer to soften the astringency or tannins in black tea by adding a dash of milk. Whether you put the milk into the cup first or add it to a full cup of tea is a matter of personal preference.

Choose lowfat or whole milk to flavor your tea. Do not use cream because it's too heavy for the delicate taste of the tea. Also don't add lemon after you've put milk into tea because that will cause the milk to curdle as well as give the tea an unpleasant taste.

EXPLORE

Experiment with a variety of ways to make your favorite teas. Be creative with the amount of tea, the water temperature and the steeping time. Keep notes on which details give you the perfect cup of tea for your taste. Your own personal preference should always be your guide to making your best cup of tea.

PART THREE

How Tea Is Good for You

Drinking a daily cup of tea will surely starve the apothecary.
– Chinese proverb

CHAPTER 6

Ways Tea Improves Your Life

On a cold, rainy Iowa afternoon, I felt kind of down and out of sorts. A challenging week had left me physically and emotionally exhausted. I even wondered if I might be getting a cold or the flu.

I thought about reading but felt restless and couldn't concentrate. I considered taking a nap but knew that might make me feel even more tired. Although I was lounging in my sweatpants and flannel shirt, I still felt cold.

As I wandered through my home, I caught sight of my favorite chair. The soft green fabric rocker had a cozy knitted afghan tossed over the back, beckoning me to sink down and rest. Suddenly, I knew exactly what I needed—a hot cup of tea!

I hurried into the kitchen and studied my tea selections. I remember hearing the phrase "a hug in a cup" used to describe a traditional English Breakfast tea. I immediately knew that was a perfect choice.

I pulled out my favorite china teapot—the tall, white one circled with delicate blue flowers—then also reached for my oversized mug. I carefully heated water to the correct temperature, poured it over the tea leaves in my teapot and let it steep for a few minutes. Then with my filled mug in my hand, I relaxed into the rocking chair, eased my legs onto the cushioned footstool and began sipping my wonderful tea.

An hour later, I realized my energy and focus had returned and I felt so much better. The tea had restored my balance in life and helped to heal my stress and anxiety. My spirit felt soothed and comforted, and I felt like myself again! I wasn't chilled anymore, and I no longer worried I was getting the flu. I also realized I had read several chapters in my novel without any concern about focusing. I had experienced the miracle of a cup of tea!

Health benefits of tea

You probably know how tea warms, soothes and energizes you. But clinical research on tea shows it also does a lot more. It provides subtle benefits such as improving brain health as well as lowering cholesterol and decreasing risk of heart disease.

Studies have also linked tea drinking with a lower risk of developing Type II diabetes and cancer. Many women even attribute having a great complexion to being an avid tea drinker.

Most of the research on the benefits of tea was done on traditional ones, including black, white and green teas. While the amounts varied quite a bit, a number of studies showed benefits for people who drank an average of just three cups of tea per day.

One interesting study showed L-theanine, an amino acid found in black tea, actually improved thinking and mental focus. Participants in the study reported feeling more productive along with having an improved ability to solve complex problems.

So if you're facing a work challenge or trying to make a hard decision about something, stop for a few minutes and drink a cup of black tea. You may find solutions to your problem suddenly become a lot clearer.

Green tea contains EGCG, a compound that reportedly boosts your immune system, lowers blood sugar and improves mental clarity. There's even a group of studies that show women who regularly drink green tea tend to have increased bone density, which lowers the risk of osteoporosis and bone fractures.

Caffeine levels

If you are trying to limit your caffeine intake, drinking tea will help you do that. But the amount of caffeine per cup depends on a number of factors. Before brewing, most tea leaves contain more caffeine than coffee beans. However, a steeped cup of tea will have much less caffeine than a brewed cup of coffee.

An 8-ounce cup of black tea contains about 50 milligrams of caffeine, which is less than half the amount in a cup of brewed coffee. Other types of tea, such as oolong and green tea, have even less caffeine per cup.

One benefit of tea is that its high levels of antioxidants slow the body's absorption of caffeine. This results in a gradual increase of caffeine in the system as well as a longer period of alertness with no crash at the end.

The factors that affect caffeine content the most are the water temperature used for brewing and the length of steeping time. So a black tea steeped for five minutes in boiling water will have a lot more caffeine than a white tea steeped for two minutes at 180°F.

Some studies have shown that the location of the leaf on the tea plant also affects the amount of caffeine in a particular tea. Interestingly, the youngest leaves, which are the highest on the plant, contain a higher concentration of caffeine as well as more beneficial antioxidants.

If you're wanting to avoid caffeine entirely, choose from the many varieties of herbal teas (tisanes) such as chamomile, hibiscus and peppermint. Unless they are combined with leaves from a traditional tea plant, herbal teas will always be caffeine free. One exception is yerba mate, which contains close to half the amount of caffeine found in a similar-sized cup of coffee.

You may be surprised to know that, unlike herbal teas, decaffeinated teas are not caffeine-free. Most tea producers use a high-pressure extraction process which removes most of the caffeine without compromising the flavor, color and quality of the teas. But even after this process, decaffeinated tea will still contain a small amount of caffeine, usually between two to six milligrams per cup.

Sharing tea with others

Perhaps more than any other common beverage, tea builds and influences our relationships. When you gather with a group of friends and sip tea together, you somehow feel closer and more connected.

Sharing tea becomes even more important when someone is going through hard times in life. The loss of a loved one, relationship struggles or recovering from illness such as cancer can leave people feeling lost and alone. Sharing the gift of tea with them can help ease the pain and bring comfort and emotional healing.

When I know a friend needs comforted or encouraged, I reach for a gift of tea and, if possible, deliver it in person. In most cases, I will sit with my friend for a while as we visit and drink tea together.

People will often discuss their thoughts and fears more easily with someone who listens over a cup of tea. For some reason, it seems easier to share pain when you share tea.

I usually try to choose a type of tea that will match a person's need, and I've found my tea gifts are always appreciated. When a friend was struggling with new medications prescribed for her heart problems, I chose a black Darjeeling tea that would help her feel stronger physically as well as emotionally.

Another friend appreciated the sturdy Earl Grey tea I brought when she was facing chemotherapy. Sometimes, just the gift alone can be comforting and healing.

A colleague told me how, during the early weeks after her breast cancer surgery, a neighbor stopped by with a pretty gift bag tied shut with a gold ribbon. Inside were two homemade scones and an assortment of her favorite teas. She told me the tea gift made her feel loved and encouraged during that very difficult time in her life.

Never underestimate the power of a cup of tea. Gather your favorite type, brew it nicely, then sip away by yourself or with a group of friends. Whenever you drink tea, remember that you are improving your health as well as your life.

EXPLORE

Plan a time to share tea with someone who needs a bit of encouragement or support. Choose a quiet setting where you can visit easily and each reveal your personal thoughts and needs. Notice how this simple ritual enhances and energizes your life.

I like a nice cup of tea in the morning for to start the day
you see, and at half past eleven, well my idea of heaven
is a nice cup of tea. I like a nice cup of tea with my dinner,
and a nice cup of tea with my tea, and when it's time for bed
there's a lot to be said for a nice cup of tea.

– A.P. Herbert, English playwright (1890-1971)

CHAPTER 7

Tea Rituals and Meditation

As you become more passionate about tea, you'll discover lots of ways to use it in your daily life. From sipping from a steaming cup soon after waking to reaching for a chilled, flavorful glass after a hectic day, tea helps you feel grounded and prepared for whatever comes next.

Over time, you'll find that tea becomes a subtle anchor in your day. It quiets your mind and brings random thoughts into focus. It also soothes your spirit after a restless night or a stressful conversation. Often you'll realize that after finishing your tea, you return to your tasks feeling renewed and refreshed.

In my own life, I follow some of the precepts of Buddhism, such as showing compassion and easing suffering for those around me. For many years, I have used meditation as a form of nurturing and mindfulness to help me with these goals.

In my early morning practice, I count on tea to help me feel centered and ready to access the deepest areas of my heart. Tea becomes the connection to my soul as it eases my tension and soothes my spirit.

Steps for a tea meditation

While there are many styles and types of meditation, my approach is quite simple. It usually includes a cup of tea, either during the meditation or enjoyed soon afterward.

I encourage you to experiment with doing a tea meditation. I prefer early morning for meditating, but you can do this at any time of day or evening.

Feel free to vary this idea to match your personal needs and style, but at least in the beginning, follow these easy steps to make it work best.

1. Plan the setting

Choose where you will sit for this meditation time. Select a chair with a table nearby where you can set your steaming cup of tea.

Once you have chosen your seating plan, remove any distractions that might interrupt quieting your mind. Close the door, silence your phone and put your pets in another room so they don't come sneaking in for attention.

Decide if you want background music or if you will meditate in silence. If you decide to use music as part of your experience, make sure it's instrumental only and played at a very soft volume.

2. Prepare your tea

Think carefully about which type of tea you will enjoy during this time. Start by doing a quick assessment of your mood. Then decide if you want a robust black or oolong tea or if your heart wants a tea that's very nurturing and soothing such as a white, yellow or green tea.

Then, depending on your tea choice, begin the steps to making it. Be sure to heat the water to the correct temperature for your specific type of tea. I own a variable temperature electric tea kettle that can be set for the perfect match of my tea. But you can also use an instant-read kitchen thermometer for this.

Once the water is hot, pour it over your tea and allow time for it to steep. Pay attention to the color of your steeped tea, from almost white or pale yellow to darker shades of green or black. When it's at the strength you prefer, pour your tea through a fine mesh strainer. If you used a tea bag, remove it before pouring your tea. Be sure to notice the delightful sound of tea being poured from the teapot into your cup.

3. Enjoy your tea and your meditation

Carry your tea to your special place and take a seat in your comfortable chair. Wrap your hands around the warm cup and inhale the aroma. Even the delightful smell of the tea becomes part of your experience.

As you carefully sip tea from your cup, close your eyes and invite your mind to become quiet and peaceful. Stay in your meditation for as long as you wish, continuing to drink the tea as part of the connection with your spirit.

My personal tea meditation

To help you visualize the steps of doing a tea meditation, here are more details on my own practice. I meditate each morning for at least 30 minutes, and it's always the first thing I do upon waking up, which is usually around six or six-thirty a.m.

Sometimes, I make tea first and hold the teacup in my hand and sip during meditation. But many times, I wait and make tea after my meditation is complete.

My favorite spot is in the library of my home, where there's a comfortable glider rocker saved from a family farm. It's partly covered by a blue and white afghan made by my aunt, and the table beside it is taller than a typical side table, so it's the perfect height for my tea.

I usually meditate in silence as I try to reach a quiet state of mind and let go of my busy "monkey mind." Whenever my thoughts stray and I start thinking about my troubles, my to-do list or other concerns, I gently bring my mind back to the quiet state.

I always sit facing east, with my eyes closed. By the end of my meditation, the sun is usually coming up in the east, and I can look out at the woods behind my house. I use the beautiful woods as a touchstone to anchor me to the beginning of my day.

Often for part of my meditation time, I visualize a tea plantation and the deep green leaves of the tea plants. I might picture rows and rows of plants ascending the hills in the tea gardens of India. I mentally listen to sounds I might hear in the tea gardens, such as the gentle voices of workers. I picture many details of this place, including the smells and the touch of the tea leaves.

My tea ritual

If I'm planning to drink tea while I'm meditating, I make the tea ritual part of my practice. First, I consider which tea to enjoy, and I actually love the anticipation of deciding on my tea each morning.

Once I've chosen a favorite tea for the day, I use my electric tea kettle to heat the water to the proper temperature for that tea. When the water is ready, I carefully fill my clear glass teapot with hot water, then watch the "agony of the leaves," the act of unfurling while the tea is steeping.

When my tea is ready, I pour it out slowly, noticing the delightful sound as it fills the cup. I move to my glider rocking chair and settle in for my practice. As I take a first sip of tea, I close my eyes and slowly begin to breathe in and out. Soon I mentally go to a quiet, soothing place, and I spend the next half hour enjoying my tea meditation.

EXPLORE

Using the steps outlined in this chapter, plan a special tea experience. If you are hesitant about the idea of meditating, simply plan a tea adventure that matches your needs.

Carefully consider the type of tea you want, then brew it, steep it and pour the finished tea into a special cup. Sit in a cozy, comfortable chair and relax as you sip your wonderful tea.

You can drink your tea while sitting in silence, but you can also enjoy it while reading, listening to music or visiting with a friend. After you finish your tea meditation or tea adventure, make notes in a journal about what you experienced, including sights, sounds, smells and thoughts.

PART FOUR

Finding Your Favorite Teas

When you have flowers, books, and tea, you are never alone.

– Alexandra Stoddard, author and
philosopher of contemporary living

CHAPTER 8

Tasting and Evaluating Tea

As you continue studying and learning about tea, you'll begin to recognize the differences in grades of tea, especially loose leaf teas. Knowing these levels will guide you in choosing high-quality teas as well as knowing which ones to skip.

As you know by now, I'm a huge fan of tea infusions made with loose leaf teas. When you make a cup of tea using loose leaf instead of tea bags, you'll find the flavors and aromas are more pronounced. These infusions will also deepen your appreciation for the many varieties of tea.

Tea cupping

Professional tea tasters use a process called "cupping," which is a method of tasting and evaluating the quality of loose leaf tea. A combination of art and science, tea cupping is used by tea lovers throughout the world to maintain tea quality and tea drinking satisfaction.

Even tea from the same shipment, tea garden or processing batch can differ in taste, and the step of tea cupping provides a way to ensure quality control. For many tea connoisseurs, knowing that a supplier properly cups its tea adds to the tea drinking experience.

Industry professionals may taste and evaluate several dozen teas during a day. Because of how tea tasting is done, the tasters end up sipping from hundreds of tablespoons of tea. As they evaluate each one, the tasters carefully monitor the sight, smell, taste and even mouthfeel of each tea.

In a manner similar to wine tasting, professional tea tasters do not drink or swallow the tea. Instead they carefully slurp and evaluate the tea, then spit it out. Slurping allows the taster to get the tea to the back of the mouth, which moves aromatic sensations of tea to the nasal passages.

Tea tasting event

A great way to enhance your knowledge of tea is to set up your own cupping or tasting event. You can do this alone, but it's even more fun if you invite a group of friends.

Begin by deciding which category of tea you'll use for your tasting. Start with the ones you enjoy the most, such as black or green tea. For another tasting event, you might branch out to tasting oolong, white or pu-erh tea.

You'll be evaluating the teas based on the same four criteria used by professional tasters: sight, smell, taste and mouthfeel. You don't need a lot of equipment for a tea tasting. All that's required is a tea kettle to heat the water, a measuring spoon or perhaps a scale to weigh the tea, shallow white plates and several white cups. You'll also want to gather a bunch of tablespoons which will be used for the actual tasting. I recommend you plan to evaluate only a few teas at each tasting, limiting it to three or four different ones.

To prepare for the tasting, line the white cups in a row on the table, then using small bags or containers, put the precise amount of measured or weighed tea behind each cup. Usually this is approximately two grams for a six- to eight-ounce cup. Place a card in front of each cup, listing the name and origin of that specific tea.

Start your tea tasting by following the steps below in order. Work with only one tea at a time so that you don't confuse the qualities of the specific teas. Evaluate these categories for each of the teas on your table.

Sight and smell

Pick up the sample of your first tea and pour the leaves onto a shallow white plate. Look carefully at the appearance of the dry leaves. Especially note the colors of the leaves, which can indicate the amount of oxidation the leaves have undergone. Check for consistent size and shape of the tea leaves. The best quality teas will have a minimum of broken leaves.

Next, pay attention to the smell of the dry tea leaves. Before you infuse the tea, smell the tea leaves in the larger tea canister or bag. Then, to release a more intense aroma, exhale onto the dry tea leaves in your white cup. The warmth of your breath will make the aroma more intense.

You can even use this technique at a tea store that has a wall of tin or glass canisters of tea. Ask the tea seller to let you smell several of the teas. To do this properly, shake the tea canister first to release the aroma, then put your nose close to the opening and inhale. Be sure to notice whether the tea has a clean, fresh aroma or if it seems a little dark or stale.

Now you are ready to infuse your tea. Using filtered water that's been heated to the correct temperature for your type of tea, pour hot water over the tea leaves. After giving them a few minutes to infuse, pour off the tea liquor and analyze the wet tea leaves. Note the size of the leaves, whether there are uniform pieces, and whether most of the leaves are still attached to a stem.

Look at the tea liquor you poured off and describe the color. Below are some general descriptions of colors based on specific categories of teas. Try to describe the color of the tea liquor as precisely as you can.

- White tea: pale to bright yellow
- Yellow tea: shades of yellow
- Green tea: pale green to bright, dark green
- Oolong tea: yellow to red
- Black tea: various shades of red and copper
- Dark tea, pu-erh: yellow to red to black

Smell the tea again after you've infused it and see if it smells the same or if the aroma has changed. Decide if you enjoy the aroma of that specific tea. See if you can match the smell to some of the aromas listed below.

- Earthy: mineral, earth, woodsy
- Vegetal: grass, cooked vegetables, herbs, dried plants
- Floral: jasmine, rose, gardenia, lilac
- Nutty: almond, pine nuts, walnut, chestnut, hazelnut
- Sweet: malt, honey, caramel, maple syrup, toffee
- Spicy: ginger, licorice, clove, vanilla, pepper, nutmeg, cinnamon
- Fruity: berries, citrus, tree or vine fruit, tropical fruits, cooked fruits

Taste and mouthfeel

Now it's time to taste the tea you've brewed. As you know, professional tea tasters spit the tea out as they taste it. You don't need to do this part if it doesn't appeal to you. Simply follow the steps for tasting but go ahead and swallow the tea in between sips.

To get the best sense of the taste and texture of your tea, take a slurp (not sip) of the hot beverage to aerate it and move it to the back of your mouth. This engages your retronasal receptors, which evaluate the smell and taste of the tea differently from other areas of your mouth.

Take another slurp and swish the tea around on your tongue to assess the taste and the body or viscosity of the tea. As tea cools, the aroma and flavor will change slightly, and eventually you will be able to recognize these subtle differences.

Each time you take a slurp, decide if you want to spit out the tea or swallow it. Either way, you'll continue to develop a more discriminating tea palate.

As you evaluate the taste of your tea, note which of the flavor sensations match what you're tasting. You are familiar with the four common tastes, which are bitter, salty, sweet and sour. Many years ago, the Japanese noted a fifth taste, which they called umami. This is more of a savory taste which can be recognized in certain types of teas.

Mouthfeel describes the viscosity or thickness of your tea. The most common ones are astringent, buttery, creamy and oily. But many teas will feel silkier or smoother, even velvety.

Complete your tea tasting by making notes in a tea tasting journal or other notebook. As you continue to explore the taste of tea, you can come back to those first experiences and see how your palate changes over time.

EXPLORE

Set up a tea tasting event, either alone or with a group of friends. Choose several variations within one category such as black or green teas. Have fun noticing the details of the sight, smell, taste and mouthfeel of each of the teas. Be sure to write some notes or record the experiences in a tea tasting journal.

There is no trouble so great or grave that cannot be much diminished by a nice cup of tea.

– Bernard-Paul Heroux, Basque philosopher

CHAPTER 9

Tea Tasting Journal

Do you have trouble remembering the name of a favorite tea? Maybe you taste a new tea that you love, but can't recall the details that made it so wonderful. It sounds like it's time for a tea tasting journal.

You can use loose pages, a small notebook or a purchased journal made for tea tasting. Whenever you try a new tea or enjoy a favorite one, simply record notes about the type of tea, the general taste, the cost per cup and any details that will help you remember what you liked about it.

By keeping a personal record of your tea experiences and adventures, you'll find it easy to go back to your favorite teas. You'll also be able to remember where you bought them and find ideas for gifting tea to others.

Start your journal entry with the date you enjoyed the tea and whether it was new to you or one you've tasted in the past. Then write notes that include as many of these details as you wish.

⋄ Tea name, brand
⋄ Type of tea (white, yellow, green, oolong, black, pu-erh, herbal)
⋄ Country of origin, perhaps the estate it came from

- ⬧ Where you purchased it, cost of the tea as well as the cost per cup (To calculate this, divide what you paid per ounce of tea by 12. This is the approximate number of cups of tea one ounce will yield. So if you paid $6 per ounce for a specialty tea, your cost comes to 50 cents a cup.)
- ⬧ Notes on the dry tea leaves, including shape, color and aroma
- ⬧ Water temperature for infusing, steeping time
- ⬧ The number of steepings and any changes such as additional steeping time
- ⬧ Notes on the infused tea including appearance, color and aroma
- ⬧ Details on the flavor of the infused tea, the mouthfeel and any aftertaste

When you finish recording the details, add any personal notes, then rank the tea using a star rating or other system to grade your tea tasting experience. Over time, you'll find these notes will guide you with tea purchases as well as choosing your favorite ones to drink.

You can find a wide variety of tea tasting journals at your favorite bookstore or online resource. At the end of this chapter, you'll find an example of a simple tea tasting journal to use as a guide. To print copies of this journal, go to my website: www. Talking-Tea.com.

Keep in mind that a tasting journal along with a tin of specialty tea makes a great birthday or holiday gift for a tea-loving friend.

EXPLORE

Invite a friend for a tea tasting party and use a tasting journal or the sample from this book to make detailed comments about the teas. Keep separate notes, then compare your experiences including how much you liked each of the teas.

Tea Tasting Journal

Date of tasting _____

Tea name and brand _____

Tea type:
☐ white ☐ yellow ☐ green ☐ oolong ☐ black ☐ pu-erh ☐ herbal

Country of origin, estate _____

Where purchased_____

Cost per bag _____ Cost per cup _____

Water temperature _____ Steeping time _____

Dry leaves: Shape, color and aroma _____

_____

Infused leaves: Appearance, color, aroma _____

_____

Infused tea: Flavor, mouthfeel, aftertaste _____

_____

Tasting Notes

_____

_____

_____

_____

_____

_____

Buy again: Yes ☐   No ☐

Ranking of this tea (five is best)

The shortest distance between two strangers is
a full teapot and two cups.
– from *365 Things Every Tea Lover Should Know*

CHAPTER 10

Tea Room Fun

Thick, white fabric covers each of the many tables in a lavishly decorated room. Vases filled with tiny pink and yellow flowers adorn the center of each table. On either side of the tall windows along one wall, cream and gold brocade drapes diffuse the bright sunshine. Soft classical music playing in the background makes the area feel calm and peaceful.

At each place setting, delicate china cups and saucers wait to be filled. A pot of tea, made of course with loose leaf tea, is set on each table, along with a three-tiered china serving tray filled with tiny sandwiches, scones and sweets.

The tea room is ready, and afternoon tea is served!

This lovely tea room could be located almost anywhere, especially in any larger city. While the settings and decorations are unique to each tea room, the basic format is similar. In most tea rooms, you will see elegant decorations, china dishes and a wonderful array of tasty foods to enjoy along with your pot of tea.

Remember the story of the English Duchess of Bedford, who began inviting her friends to enjoy tea and snacks in her home?

Over many years, this trend grew, and "taking tea" became a fashionable afternoon ritual. I hope you have enjoyed taking tea at a formal tea room somewhere and, if not, I encourage you to put that on the list for your next travel adventure.

Tea room visits

You can find many styles of tea rooms, from high-end, formal settings in hotel restaurants to small cozy spaces in shops that sell crafts and tea wares. I have visited all kinds of tea rooms, often with friends or family members, and I have special memories from each of them. In fact, when I look at photos or bring up images of these visits, I can instantly relive the occasions and feel the warmth of these special times.

For many years, whenever I would travel to see my son and family in New York City, my daughter-in-law, Preethi, and I would plan to visit a new tea room. From every corner of Manhattan, Brooklyn and other areas of New York, we've taken tea in everything from elegant venues to small, intimate tea shops.

On one of these visits, my husband and son joined us for a traditional afternoon tea at Lady Mendl's, which is a chic tea salon located in historical Gramercy Park. The menu included a five-course tea service with soup or salad and a selection of traditional tea sandwiches and scones, along with sweets including crepes and petit fours. We each had our own pot of tea, and we ended our delightful afternoon lunch with champagne cocktails.

The following morning, my son and I had breakfast at one of the Alice's Teacup locations in Manhattan. Under strings of tiny white lights, we enjoyed a leisurely meal of omelets and breakfast potatoes along with great conversation over a pot of Alice's Breakfast Tea. Of course, we couldn't resist taking a scone to go!

On another New York trip, Preethi arranged for us to attend a private tasting of five Taiwanese oolong teas at the tiny Te Company. Before the shop opened for business that day, the young woman who owns it educated us about several of her favorite oolongs. She explained how once a year, when she goes home to visit her parents in Taiwan, she meets in person with tea farmers and purchases her teas directly from them.

In addition to tasting and learning about the five oolong teas, we nibbled on snacks made by the shop owner's husband, who is a Portuguese chef. For his wife's tea shop, he has created a specialty cookie made with two discs of hazelnut shortbread with a spicy pineapple filling. They are topped with a few grains of coarse salt and some lime zest. Best of all, you can purchase these amazing cookies from the shop's online store.

Tea room menus

Whether at a formal hotel in a big city or a tiny restaurant in a semi-rural area, tea rooms tend to follow similar patterns. Menus will vary a lot, but most tea rooms include these basic offerings for an afternoon tea:

- A pot of tea for each guest, with a choice of the type of tea
- A selection of tiny sandwiches or appetizers
- Scones served with jam and Devonshire or clotted cream
- Pastries that include cakes, cookies, shortbread and sweets
- Option of adding a glass of champagne or a bubbly cocktail

Most afternoon tea menus include dainty sandwiches made from soft bread with the crusts cut off. The sandwich fillings will often be egg or chicken salad or the famous cucumber slices with herbed cream cheese. And with dozens of ways to make scones, you might be served ones that include fruit, spices or flavorful additions, such as pumpkin.

What makes a scone extra tasty is the clotted cream and jam. While thick strawberry jam is most typical, you might also be served a variety of other flavors. Clotted cream, also called Devonshire cream, is made by gently cooking heavy cream to give it a thick, smooth consistency similar to butter. The blend of the jam and clotted cream on a scone creates a flavor burst that most people love.

In some tea rooms, lemon curd is served with the scones. This delicious dessert spread is made with lemon juice, sugar, butter and eggs. If you are a fan of the taste of lemon, you will swoon over this scone topping.

Tea room memories

Some years ago, my husband and I traveled to Victoria, British Columbia, where we enjoyed a civilized afternoon tea at the iconic Fairmont Empress Hotel. My sister, Sue, and her husband joined us at this famous hotel, which has served a traditional British-style afternoon tea since 1908.

The set-price menu included our choice of several tea flavors and, of course, the traditional three-tiered stand with a selection of delicious savory and sweet snacks. We especially loved the wonderful scones served with traditional clotted cream and jam.

We sat across from each other on comfortable couches and listened to the soft piano music in the background while a tea sommelier in an impeccable black suit served our tea and delicacies. For an additional charge, we added a lovely glass of champagne at the end of our tea!

After the tea, we shopped at the hotel gift shop, and I brought home a black shirt with a sparkly blue, silver and rose teacup on the front. Every time I wear that shirt, I remember how much I enjoyed that special day with some of my favorite people.

In San Diego, my daughter-in-law, Amy, and I have enjoyed afternoon tea several times at the Julian Tea and Cottage Arts. In 2003, this delightful restaurant and store was miraculously spared from harm when a massive wildfire destroyed more than 270,000 acres very close to the historic mining town of Julian.

The Julian tea room sells beautiful teapots and cups as well as a large selection of teas. Since lilacs are my favorite flower, I especially treasure the lilac pattern Staffordshire teapot I purchased on one of my visits there.

Of course, it's never too early to help the next generation learn about the tradition of fancy afternoon tea. On another San Diego trip, my friends, Jeanne and Delia, and I visited the Coral Tree Tea House in Old Town's historic Victorian Heritage Park. Jane, my 12-year-old granddaughter, joined us for a classic English-style tea with sandwiches, apple Waldorf salad and the chef's dessert. She loved it and told me she wants to enjoy afternoon tea a lot in the years ahead.

Unusual tea room visits

I've had afternoon tea experiences in every setting from formal hotels to tiny spaces in an alley. Each one has given me a unique adventure and a new set of wonderful memories.

My most unusual tea room adventure didn't even take place in a tea room! On one of my trips to New York, my daughter-in-law and I planned a visit to Ippodo, a matcha tea room in a small townhouse on a side street in Lower Manhattan. When we reached the store, we were disappointed to discover there was no seating, and the matcha tea drinks were only offered to-go.

But we went ahead and ordered, then watched with fascination while the young man behind the counter whipped our matcha drinks using a chasen, which is a traditional bamboo whisk. After he finished, we walked across the street with our to-go cups of matcha, then sat on a doorstep and had a lovely spontaneous chat.

Another unusual experience was a visit along with our long-time friends, Roger and Sandy, to the Imperial Tea Court in San Francisco. Owned by Roy and Grace Fong, this well-known venue was the first traditional Chinese teahouse in the United States.

An ordained Taoist priest, Mr. Fong strives to honor the ancient rites of tea, and he demonstrated how to steep our tea in a gaiwan, a ceramic lidded cup used to steep tea in China. I was so impressed that before I left his shop, I purchased a beautiful yellow gaiwan decorated with red flowers and green vines.

Finding tea rooms

The venues I've mentioned are just a few examples of the hundreds of places where you can enjoy a delightful afternoon tea. I encourage you to look for tea rooms in your own area as well as in cities and towns you visit in your travels.

You can search online for tea rooms, afternoon tea or even tea shops, since many of these include a small restaurant. Soon, you might add an entirely new requirement to your vacations—the opportunity to enjoy tea and conversation in a wonderful tea room.

If you visit a tea room that includes a gift shop, be sure to purchase some special teas or tea wares to take home. Often you can find beautiful teapots, plates, cups and other unique tea-related items. Each time you use these, you'll bring up memories of your tea room visits as well as your special times with friends or family.

I often look for tea-themed gifts such as note cards, stationery, books or small tea wares that I can give to family or friends after I return home.

I also love receiving tea-related gifts, and one of my favorites is the tea calendar my friend, Helen, gives me every year for my birthday. It hangs on the wall inside my library where I see it several times a day. Each month on this calendar features a unique picture of a beautiful teapot and delicious tea treats. That gift always inspires me when I look out the window at the woods while I sit and meditate or work at my computer.

EXPLORE

Whenever you're traveling with friends or family members, seek out a tea room venue that offers a special afternoon tea. Dress up, wear a hat and practice good tea etiquette as you quietly sip your tea. Notice the quality of conversation that flows during your visit in a tea room setting.

Because tea rooms frequently change hours or are open only a few days a week, be sure to check for details about hours of operation and the need for reservations.

For more information on popular tea rooms, see my website: www.Talking-Tea.com.

PART FIVE

A Short Tea Education

Wouldn't it be dreadful to live in a country
where they didn't have tea?

– Sir Noel Coward, English playwright and composer
(1899-1973)

CHAPTER 11

Where Tea Comes From

You gently hold a steaming cup of tea, then lift it to your lips for that first sip. *Ahhh.* That is so nice. As usual, your tea represents many things—calming, nurturing, energizing, soothing, even fun.

Do you ever wonder where the tea in your cup came from? I don't mean which grocery store or specialty shop. I'm talking about the ground where the tea plant took in rain and sunshine, then produced the tea leaves that created your wonderful cup of tea.

The type and flavor of your tea might give you some clues about where it came from. Most black or traditional teas grow best in areas with consistently warm temperatures and high humidity. Tea plants also require a lot of water, so they do well in countries with a high annual rainfall.

Most of the tea you drink comes from either China or India. But surprisingly, you might also be enjoying tea from Africa, Sri Lanka, Turkey or even Vietnam.

Tea in the United States

In the late 19th century, Dr. Charles Shephard established the Pinehurst Tea Plantation in South Carolina. Sometime later, the tea plants were moved to a research station on Wadmalaw Island off the coast of South Carolina.

This amazing tea plantation was briefly owned by Lipton before it was sold to a private company that produced American Classic Tea. In 2003, Bigelow purchased the 40-acre tea estate and renamed it Charleston Tea Plantation.

If you want an adventure along with a great tea education, plan a visit to this famous tea company. Charleston Tea Plantation is the only one in North America where you can see hundreds of thousands of tea bushes stretching out acre after acre for almost as far as the eye can see.

In addition to displaying acres of tea plants, the plantation offers an educational tour of its tea factory. You get to walk the entire length of the tea production building, where you can see all the equipment needed to make tea.

First flush tea

The Charleston Tea Plantation also lets you sign up to purchase first flush tea. The term "first flush" is defined as the new growth of leaves on the tea plants in the springtime after they awaken from dormancy. This usually happens in April or May, and it creates a unique taste available only once during a growing season. As a true tea connoisseur, you can impress your friends with this knowledge even if you never purchase the tea.

Top ten tea-producing countries

The Resources section in this book includes a detailed listing of specific types of teas and the countries that grow and produce them. This will help you learn which locations grow your favorite kinds of teas.

Here's a listing of the ten countries that produce the most tea. The next time you buy tea, study the label or research the tea online to see where it was grown and produced

Rank	Country	Annual Production (Tons)
1	China	2,414,802
2	India	1,252,174
3	Kenya	473,000
4	Sri Lanka	349,308
5	Turkey	243,000
6	Vietnam	240,000
7	Indonesia	144,015
8	Argentina	89,609
9	Japan	80,200
10	Iran	75,000

Source: 2018 Food and Agriculture Organization (FAO)

EXPLORE

Expand your knowledge of tea by exploring one specific type, such as black tea. To do this, locate and purchase black teas from two or three countries, such as Sri Lanka, India and Nepal. You may need to go to a specialty tea store or online resource to find these teas.

As you drink each of these teas, make notes about the differences between each of them. Over time, you will begin to differentiate and identify the specific black teas from each of these countries.

What better way to suggest friendliness – and to create it –
than with a cup of tea?

– J. Grayson Luttrell, around 1940, vice president
McCormick & Company

CHAPTER 12

Where to Buy Good Quality Tea

As you continue your journey to becoming a tea connoisseur, you will start to develop a taste for higher quality teas. Soon you'll be searching for new types and varieties of your favorite ones.

Knowing where to buy high-quality tea will add to your shopping fun as well as to your appreciation of the teas themselves. You don't need to stop buying teas at your grocery store. In fact, that's a good place to branch out and try new types and flavors of tea.

Study the brands in the tea and coffee aisle and experiment with ones you haven't tried before. Make notes in your tea tasting journal to help you remember your new favorites. But when you get tired of tea bags and want more adventure with your teas, look for places where you can find loose leaf teas.

If you live close to specialty stores such as Whole Foods, explore the larger selection of loose leaf teas. Buy a couple new ones, properly brew and steep one of them, then hold the cup of tea in your hand as you focus on enjoying a new flavor and kind of tea.

When you're ready to experiment even more, plan to visit an actual tea store. Ideally, go to one of these stores in person, where you can see, smell and taste several varieties of tea. Some larger stores host tea classes or tastings that focus on one specific type of tea, such as oolong.

Eventually, you'll reach a point of being willing to purchase specialty teas online and have them shipped to you. Once you find vendors you like and trust, making tea purchases this way will become a lot easier. With online purchases, it's best to buy often and in small amounts. This helps you to always enjoy fresh teas and maintain a supply of high-quality ones.

Cost of a cup of tea

When you first consider buying tea at specialty retail and online tea stores, it might seem rather expensive. But here's a way to always put the price of tea into perspective.

Most tea stores sell loose leaf tea by the ounce, usually with the option of purchasing either two or four ounces of a tea at a time. Suppose you pay $25 for a four-ounce bag of a wonderful tea. With most loose leaf teas, a four-ounce bag will yield approximately 50 cups of tea.

To calculate your cost per cup, divide the $25 price of the tea by 50, and you will realize that you are paying just 50 cents for each cup of tea. This amounts to a fraction of what you would pay for a specialty drink at your local coffee shop. And many good quality loose leaf teas are available for considerably less than $25 per bag.

As you discover your favorite online sellers, pay attention to how they price their teas. In addition to a specific number of ounces, many stores also offer a "tasting" amount for very little cost. And along with your tea purchase, some vendors will include a small free sample of another tea.

Tea stores online

Here are some of my favorite online stores where you can count on receiving good quality teas. With time, you'll build your own list of shops and know which teas you prefer from each one.

Many of these vendors have retail locations as well an online store. Whenever you are close to one of the retail stores, try to plan a visit and buy teas in person.

Gong Fu Tea

The owners of this retail store in Des Moines, Iowa, define Gong Fu Tea as a venue for tea enthusiasts everywhere. Their goal is to source the very finest quality teas and tea wares available, backed by dependable, expert service and a 100% guarantee. They offer both a retail store and a great online shop.

www.gongfu-tea.com

TeaSource

This wonderful store is located in Roseville, Minnesota. To help you choose from their overwhelming number of teas, they have an online tea quiz that helps you find ones you'll enjoy.

www.teasource.com

Palais des Thés

While the main store is located in Paris, this company has a boutique in New York City where it offers tea tastings and classes, as well as locations that serve exquisite afternoon tea.

us.palaisdesthes.com/en_us

The Tea Spot

This Colorado company focuses on "spreading wellness through tea." The founder, Maria Uspenski, is a cancer survivor who believes tea is a powerful and therapeutic elixir. The website offers a wonderful selection of teas as well as an educational and inspiring blog.

www.theteaspot.com

Rishi Tea and Botanicals

This unique Milwaukee company is a great source for organic teas. The owners travel extensively every year to find the best sources for their specialty teas.

www.rishi-tea.com

The Cultured Cup

At their retail store in Farmers Branch, Texas, the owners hold regular tea tastings that help people discover new and amazing teas. They also offer a great supply of teas available for purchase online. This store is a good source for selected Mariage Frères teas from the famous Parisian tea company by that name.

www.theculturedcup.com

In Pursuit of Tea

In addition to selling a wide variety of single-source teas, this site offers some wonderful gift sets to inspire your tea-drinking friends.

www.inpursuitoftea.com

One more way to learn about teas is to sign up for a monthly gift box or special tea shipment. Many of the stores listed above offer a Tea of the Month package or gift box.

Sips By is a great resource for monthly teas as well as options for personalized special tea boxes. The store gives you an excellent way to experiment with new teas you might not try otherwise.

https://www.sipsby.com

Here are a few more of my favorite retail and online places to buy tea. I encourage you to experiment with many of the stores listed in this chapter and build your own list of preferred tea sources.

Argo	www.argotea.com
Art of Tea	www.artoftea.com
Camellia Sinensis	www.camellia-sinensis.com
Elmwood Inn Fine Teas	www.elmwoodinn.com
Harney & Sons	www.harney.com
Ippodo Tea	www.ippodotea.com
Seven Cups	www.sevencups.com
Simpson & Vail	www.svtea.com
Single Origin Teas	www.singleoriginteas.com
Steven Smith	www.smithtea.com
Te Company	www.tecompanytea.com
Tea Gschwendner	www.shoptgtea.com
Yunnan Sourcing	www.yunnansourcing.com

EXPLORE

To grow your knowledge of tea, buy a specific type, such as a green tea, from two online vendors and compare the teas. Another time, order a full-bodied black tea, such as an Assam, from two vendors and compare the teas. Besides finding which teas you like best, you can also compare the shopping experiences with different online companies.

Tea tempers the spirit and harmonizes the mind;
dispels lassitude and relieves fatigue, awakens thought and
prevents drowsiness.
– Lu Yu, author of *The Classic of Tea* (733-804 CE)

CHAPTER 13

Mastering Tea Terms

As you can tell, I have a deep passion for tea and have studied it extensively. But as I continue to learn more about tea, my love for the subject keeps growing deeper.

A couple years ago, at the Midwest Tea Festival in Kansas City, Missouri, I attended the Tea Sommelier Training with renowned author and tea expert, James Norwood Pratt. On completion of the session, I received a Tea Sommelier Level 1 certificate, which I now proudly display on the wall in my library.

When I visited Mr. Pratt's table in the exhibit hall, I felt honored to be able to speak with him personally. As we talked, I mentioned that I would like to buy a copy of his book, *The Tea Dictionary*. I was rather surprised when he asked, "Are you sure? It's a little expensive, and I want to be sure you know that before you buy it."

I assured him that I absolutely wanted it, regardless of cost. I told him I would be adding it to my bookshelf of more than 300 books on tea that I've collected over the past 25 years.

At that point, Mr. Pratt reached out, grasped both of my hands in his, and exclaimed, "Oh my! You are one of us!" I will always remember that moment and treasure that special memory. And without hesitation, I paid more than $100 for a copy of his famous book.

Tea leaf grades

As you become a tea expert, you'll want to know which grade of tea you are buying and drinking. In the tea industry, tea leaf grading is used to evaluate products based on the quality and condition of the tea leaves themselves.

After tea is plucked, withered, oxidized and dried, the tea leaves are sorted by size of the leaf and appearance. This grading of the leaves is done in preparation for packaging and shipping to markets. Green and black teas generally have different grading systems, and the systems can vary depending on the country where the tea is manufactured.

Most black teas are graded and sold according to leaf or particle size. Harvesting and manufacturing methods affect the finished size of the leaf as well as the grade of the tea. Although many factors influence tea quality, the size and wholeness of the leaves have the most influence on the taste, clarity and brewing time.

The most common grades of tea include whole-leaf, broken leaf, fannings and dust. Within each of these grades, experts divide teas into many distinctive categories. You may see some of these listed on the packages of high-quality teas.

When tea leaves are crushed to make bagged teas, the broken leaves are referred to as CTC, which means crush-tear-curl. These lower grades of tea include fannings and dust, which are tiny remnants created in the sorting and crushing of the leaves. The majority of tea bags include fannings and dust because they provide a quick, strong infusion.

Green tea leaf grades

There is no uniform grading system for green teas, which makes it difficult for tea vendors and consumers. Chinese green teas are usually identified by a number of factors including place of origin, time of the pluck, the manufactured shape of the leaf and the season of harvest. The plucking standard, which depends on the combination of buds and leaves plucked, can also affect the tea grade. Some vendors use the designation "imperial" for top grades of green teas while others use the term "premium."

In China, teas are usually graded by number, with "first" being the highest grade, down to 7, 8 or 9, based on leaf style and shape and how carefully the manufacturing process has been carried out.

Green teas grown in Taiwan and Japan are often graded as Extra Choicest, Choicest, Choice, Finest, Fine, Good Medium, Medium, Good Common, Common, Fannings and Dust.

Black tea leaf grades

Black teas have the most complex grading system and are traditionally categorized as "whole-leaf" and "broken leaf" grades. "Fannings" and "dust" are the lowest grades as well as the least expensive teas.

Whole leaf grades

P (Pekoe): leaf that is lesser quality, no buds
OP (Orange Pekoe): young, thin, tightly rolled leaves
FOP (Flowery Orange Pekoe): finest harvest, terminal bud and two top leaves
GFOP (Golden Flowery Orange Pekoe): FOP with some golden tips
TGFOP (Tippy Golden Flowery Orange Pekoe): GFOP with many golden tips

FTGFOP (Finest Tippy Golden Flowery Orange Pekoe): FOP of excellent quality

SFTGFOP (Special Finest Tippy Golden Flowery Orange Pekoe): FOP of extraordinary quality, usually a grade reserved for first flush Darjeelings

Broken leaf grades

BOP (Broken Orange Pekoe): larger pieces of broken leaves

FBOP (Flowery Broken Orange Pekoe): includes some tips

GBOP (Golden Broken Orange Pekoe): uneven leaves and a few tips

TGFBOP (Tippy Golden Flowery Broken Orange Pekoe): high-quality leaves, many tips

Crushed Leaves

Fannings: flat pieces of tea smaller than broken; results in a stronger tea infusion

Dust: tiny particles of broken leaves; grade used only in tea bags for rapid infusion

Orange pekoe

For Western and South Asian teas, the largest of the unbroken black tea leaves are referred to as "orange pekoe." Surprisingly, "orange" has nothing to do with color, aroma or flavor of the tea. Instead, the word is used to describe a tea grade based on the size of a long unbroken leaf and its location on the tea plant.

Pekoe (which is pronounced like "gecko") refers to the down-like hairs on the youngest and smallest tea leaves on the plant. Generally, the term "orange pekoe" refers to a basic, medium-grade black tea containing many whole tea leaves. Within this category, teas can be graded into dozens of variations, mostly based on the proportion of whole leaves to smaller leaf tips or broken leaves.

If you see the word "tippy," it means the tea contains a generous amount of whole-leaf tips. For example, a good grade of black tea might be described as "Tippy Golden Flowery Orange Pekoe." Since it contains a high proportion of whole-leaf tips, this grade would be common with teas such as Darjeeling and Assam.

If you visit a shop that sells a lot of tea varieties, please don't request a "plain old orange pekoe tea." The owners will secretly smile when you aren't looking. Instead, you can ask about one of their better quality orange pekoe teas with an abundance of whole-leaf tips. You'll immediately be guided toward teas that have a lot of depth, good aroma and a pleasing taste.

Types of tea

The next section in this book provides details about the six primary classes of teas as well as the category of herbal teas and tisanes. Each chapter presents details about a specific class of tea along with examples of two unique teas of that type.

Note that, in the tea descriptions in this book, the English name is listed first, followed by the Chinese or proper name.

Here are the classes of teas:

- ⋄ White teas
- ⋄ Yellow teas
- ⋄ Green teas
- ⋄ Oolong teas
- ⋄ Black teas
- ⋄ Pu-erh teas
- ⋄ Herbal teas and tisanes

As you read about each of the specific categories, go back and review the *Periodic Table of TalkingTea* printed at the beginning of this book. It will help you follow the progression and varieties contained within each type and class of tea.

The resources section at the end of this book provides an extensive listing of 48 special teas that includes the origin, harvesting and production of each type of tea. You'll learn the names of special teas for each category, as well as some of my favorite teas of that type. I strongly encourage you to purchase only loose leaf teas as you experiment with each new type of tea.

EXPLORE

Just for fun, open a tea bag and pour the contents out onto a small plate. Notice the tiny particles. This tea dust or fannings are the result of CTC (crush-tear-curl) tea processing and are usually of lesser quality than loose leaf tea. With tea bags, the tea will infuse quickly, often resulting in a more bitter or astringent taste.

Now, put a teaspoon of loose leaf tea on the plate beside the dust or fannings and notice the difference. Some loose leaf teas are tightly curled, while others have flat, needle-like leaves. Compare the appearance, color and aroma of the two teas on the plate. If you feel adventurous, brew a pot of tea with each type and decide which one tastes better to you.

PART SIX

Specific Types of Teas

There is a great deal of poetry and fine sentiment
in a chest of tea.

Ralph Waldo Emerson, American essayist and poet (1803-1882)

CHAPTER 14

White Teas

On a day when you want to enjoy a light but healthy beverage, consider having a cup of white tea. Delicate and a little sweet tasting, white tea is made from tea leaves that are younger and less processed than green or black teas. While the taste is soft and light, the distinct characteristics of white tea make it easy to get hooked on it.

White tea gets its name from the downy white hairs on the leaves. Because this type of tea is so minimally processed, it provides a very full-bodied tea once it's infused.

White teas also contain higher levels of antioxidants than other teas. With health benefits such as decreasing inflammation and helping with digestion, white tea is a great choice for early morning or after meals.

Sources differ on the amount of caffeine in white tea, but most agree that when it is steeped at a low temperature for a short time, it will contain lower amounts of caffeine than most other teas.

You'll see white teas listed in the first row of the *Periodic Table of TalkingTea* printed at the beginning of this book.

Here are two unique white teas from Fujian, China. Originally white teas were grown only in the Fujian province, but now they are produced in several other countries as well.

See the resources section for a longer listing of white teas along with more details about each tea.

White Tip Silver Needle
Bai Hao Yin Zhen

From the Fujian province in China, this tea has an air-dried, white leaf that looks like silver needles. It is usually picked by hand only two days a year, sometime between March 15 and April 10. There is very little produced, making this tea the most expensive of traditional bud-style white teas.

White Peony
Bai Mu Dan

This rare air-dried white tea from the Fujian province has very small buds covered in silvery down. Harvested in early spring, each tea picking includes one shoot and two open leaves. White Peony tea is less expensive than Silver Needle and has a more intense flavor.

EXPLORE

If you're feeling adventurous, consider making a White Tea Martini. Here's a recipe from the book *Infused* by Henrietta Lovell:

Mix one heaping teaspoon of White Silver Tip or White Peony tea with two ounces of gin. Stir it around a bit so the leaves are submerged in the alcohol, then let it sit for about five minutes. Meanwhile, chill a glass with some ice and a little water.

After five minutes, strain the tea-infused gin into your chilled, ice-filled glass. Use a spoon to gently stir the gin and ice, gradually chilling and diluting the drink. Sip this tasty beverage slowly and enjoy your white tea martini.

A proper tea is much nicer than a very nearly tea,
which is one you forget about afterwards.
– A.A. Milne, author of *Winnie-the-Pooh* (1882-1956)

CHAPTER 15

Yellow Teas

Yellow tea, which takes its name from its straw-colored liquor, grows in the mountain regions of the Anhui and Sichuan provinces in China. Because this tea takes a lot of time and work to produce, it is China's rarest variety of loose leaf tea.

The yellow tea leaves are plucked in early spring when they are plump and juicy. After basket or pan-frying, the leaves are steamed, then smothered with a cloth. Called "sealing yellow," this step gently oxidizes the leaves before finish firing, a drying method that enhances the flavor of the tea.

The smothering process encourages the leaves to reabsorb their aromas into the buds, which creates a more aromatic and mature tea. It also helps yellow tea avoid the "grassy" taste and astringency found in many green teas.

Because yellow tea is hard to find, take extra care when purchasing it. Sometimes, a poor quality green tea is sold as yellow tea, so it's best to purchase this tea from a reputable vendor who deals directly with a tea estate in China.

Since they are so rare, yellow teas are typically not carried in supermarkets or even retail tea stores. But you can find them in a number of reputable online stores. Here are a couple of good sources for purchasing yellow teas:

www.imperialtea.com
www.yunnansourcing.com

You will find yellow teas listed in the second row of the *Periodic Table of TalkingTea* printed at the beginning of this book.

Here are two unique yellow teas. See the resources section for a longer listing of yellow teas along with more details about each tea.

Silver Needle
Jun Shan Yin Zhen

This rare tea from Hunan, China, undergoes smothering under a damp cloth, which causes a slight oxidation and gives the leaves a yellow tinge. This yellow tea is generally expensive due to very limited production.

Yellow Sprouting
Huo Shan Huang Ya

The production process of this tea blocks enzymes that cause oxidation and causes the young shoots to turn yellow. The beautiful leaves are a mixture of jade green, yellow and white colors. Single small leaves with hairy tips give this nutty and smooth tea a gentle, sweet finish.

EXPLORE

Search for a yellow tea that you can purchase in a small amount. Brew and steep it carefully, then sip it slowly. Compare the taste to other teas you have tried, then record your insights in your tea tasting journal.

Drinking tea punctuates our day with precious and refreshing pauses, whether it is after a satisfying meal or when taking a much-needed break in our busy schedule.

– Mutsuko Tokunaga, author of *New Tastes in Green Tea*
(1934-2007)

CHAPTER 16

Green Teas

Some years ago, I attended the World Tea Expo in Las Vegas. The speaker at one of the sessions talked about the growing interest in green tea for its health benefits. He then described how, on the trip from the airport to the Expo venue, his cab driver was surprised to learn that there was an entire conference devoted to tea.

The driver then enthusiastically told how his doctor had talked about the health benefits of green tea and recommended he consider drinking it. When the cab driver switched from drinking coffee to drinking green tea, he began to feel better physically as well as mentally. It appears that tea lovers and industry leaders can do market research anywhere, even in a cab from the airport!

Extolled for many health benefits, green tea has become a popular beverage in recent years. While this tea originated in China, its production and manufacture have spread to several other countries in East Asia. Known for its vegetal and refreshing flavor, green tea is made from leaves and buds that have not undergone the oxidation process used for oolong and black teas.

Production steps for green tea include careful pan-firing or steaming to stop oxidation. This is followed by a short period of high heat withering, then rolling or shaping and, finally, drying by one of several methods. This unique process locks in the flavors that will be released only when the tea is steeped in hot, not boiling water.

Keep this in mind whenever you drink green tea. If your tea tastes flat or bitter, you probably steeped it in water that was too hot.

Here are two unique green teas. See the resources section for a longer listing of green teas along with more details about each one. While there are hundreds of styles of green tea, this list includes some of the most popular ones that also are easy to find.

Remember to review the *Periodic Table of TalkingTea* printed at the beginning of this book. You'll see green teas listed in the third and fourth rows.

Green Snail Spring
Bi Luo Chun

One of China's most famous teas, this rare tea has a snail-like appearance. Once picked, the leaves and buds are rolled by hand to form tiny spirals, then fired by hot air. Because of the leaf's delicacy, water for steeping should be cooler than 175°F. I suggest you add the leaves to water, rather than pouring water onto the leaves, because that will prevent the tea from developing an astringent taste.

Dragonwell
Long Jing

Produced mostly by hand, Long Jing tea is renowned for its high quality. One of China's Ten Famous Teas, Long Jing was mentioned in the first book dedicated to tea, *The Classic of Tea*, by Lu Yu, which dates to the Tang Dynasty in approximately 760 CE.

EXPLORE

Taste one of the most common green teas, such as Gunpowder or Dragonwell. Drink it a few times until you have a feel for the taste, aroma and flavor of the tea. Then try a more expensive green tea and note the subtle differences in the color of the tea liquor, the aroma and the flavor. Add a few notes about this to your tea tasting journal.

Tea beckons us to enjoy quality time with friends and loved ones, and especially to rediscover the art of relaxed conversation.

Dorothea Johnson, author of *Tea & Etiquette: Taking Tea for Business and Pleasure*

CHAPTER 17

Oolong Teas

A few years ago, I visited the Bates Nut Farm near San Diego, California. Originally a walnut farm, this amazing venue has been owned by the Bates family for over 80 years. The owners now sell nuts from all over the world, as well as dried fruit, chocolates and other gourmet foods in their large retail space. Children love playing in the Farm Zoo and families can enjoy picnics on the grounds.

In the gourmet foods section, I found a great selection of teas, including one named milk oolong which I hadn't seen before. Since I'm not a milk drinker, I was hesitant to try this unusual tea. But as I studied the tea description, I learned that milk is not used in its production. Instead, this Taiwanese tea has a natural milky taste as a result of extra oxidation.

When I tasted the tea, I was amazed at the soft, luscious taste and quickly added this tea to my collection of favorite oolongs. Some producers create artificial milk oolong through additives, so if you decide to try it, make sure you purchase one with the natural creamy scent and flavor of milk.

Oolong, sometimes referred to as wulong, is a celebrated style of tea with great diversity and complexity. Although some tea drinkers describe oolong as "somewhere between a green and black tea," that's a rather simplified explanation. Oolong tea is made from the same plant used to make those teas, but the difference is in how the tea is processed.

While green tea is not allowed to oxidize much, black tea is left to oxidize until it turns black. Oolong tea falls somewhere in between the two, so it is partially oxidized, which results in oolong tea's color and characteristic taste.

The labor-intensive production of oolong tea includes bruising the tea leaves, which is a step unique to processing oolongs. After roasting and drying, the leaves are lightly rolled or tumbled to bruise the edges. This causes cell damage and starts the process of oxidation. Oolongs range in oxidation from 12-80%.

Here are two unique oolong teas. See the resources section for a longer listing of oolong teas along with more details about each tea.

You will find oolong teas listed in the fifth row of the *Periodic Table of TalkingTea* printed at the beginning of this book.

Iron Goddess of Mercy
Ti Kuan Yin

This oolong tea is called "monkey picked" because it's grown in hard-to-reach locations. The leaves of this tea are brilliant green and grow tightly rolled to form pearls. This oolong tea is one of China's Ten Most Famous teas.

White Tip or Oriental Beauty
Bai Hao

Originally called Formosa oolong, this is Taiwan's premier oolong tea and has quite limited production. This prized tea is usually served in small porcelain cups. You may also find it called Champagne oolong.

EXPLORE

Select one oolong tea from China and one from Taiwan, then put a teaspoon of dry leaves from each of them on a small, white plate. Compare the size of the leaves, the tightness of the rolled tea buds and the color of the tea leaves.

Now put the tea leaves into cups, pour hot water on both sets and let the leaves relax a minute. Then drain the teas and pour hot water on the tea leaves a second time. Infuse for the length of time suggested for each tea. Compare the aromas, the colors and the flavors of the two infused teas.

Happiness, in my judgment, enters the room with the tea tray.
– Thomas De Quincy, English essayist (1785-1859)

CHAPTER 18

Black Teas

In the late 1880s, my great-grandparents came to the United States from the Ostfriesland area of Germany. This area is known for its tea-blending companies and the fact that the people drink more tea per capita than in any other part of Germany.

Some years ago, my husband and I traveled to Ostfriesland and visited the manor house where my great-grandparents worked as hired hands before they emigrated. The house is now a bed and breakfast, and we stayed in a lovely blue and yellow room in a wing of the home. I loved the beauty of this area so much that I brought home a couple of traditional Ostfriesland teapots and a beautiful set of blue and white teacups. I think of my great-grandparents each time I use these for afternoon tea.

During our visit, we also learned about the traditional way people from this area drink tea. After strong black tea is brewed, the host places a piece of rock sugar into the bottom of the cup and slowly pours the tea over it. Then using a flat, shell-like spoon, the host gently pours a small amount of cream down the side of the cup. The host does not stir the tea, but lets the cream hit the bottom and mushroom up, creating a small cloud in the tea.

I also learned that in Ostfriesland, you have to put the spoon into the cup when you've had enough tea. Otherwise you will get one cup after the other. Some people end up drinking dozens of cups of tea only because they don't know how to stop it!

Since it's the most popular tea in the U.S., you probably drank black tea long before you experimented with other types of teas. Black teas go through a complete oxidation during production, which gives them a bold flavor and long shelf life. In general, most black teas have a darker color and stronger flavor than other teas.

Some black teas have been blended to create distinct taste profiles and assure the flavor is standard from year to year. For example, English Breakfast is made with a blend of teas from Assam, Sri Lanka and Kenya. Irish Breakfast has a strong Assam component, giving it a malty flavor. The most popular blended black tea, Earl Grey, is a combination of black tea and bergamot, a Mediterranean citrus fruit.

In the Resources section, I've included a list of the most popular types and varieties of black teas. Remember to review the *Periodic Table of TalkingTea* at the beginning of this book, where you'll see black teas listed in the sixth row.

Here are two of my favorite black teas.

Darjeeling
The Champagne of Teas

India's most celebrated tea, this fully oxidized, hand-picked black tea is grown in the mountains outside of the town of Darjeeling, which is in the northern state of West Bengal.

Long, cold winters and cool, breezy summers provide the ideal climate for this high-mountain tea. The cool, thin air slows leaf growth, which results in smaller leaves with a more concentrated flavor. Darjeeling teas are hand-cultivated and produced with a tremendous level of care, experience and expertise.

Assam
Camellia sinensis assamica

This fully oxidized black tea is grown on both sides of the Brahamaputra Valley in India, the birthplace of India's indigenous tea bush. The native tea tree was discovered by the British in this northeast corner of India, 120 miles east of Darjeeling. This valley is the single largest tea-growing region in the world.

A classic Indian tea with full-bodied taste, Assam tea is commonly blended into breakfast teas, including Irish Breakfast and English Breakfast. All of these teas taste great with a splash of milk.

EXPLORE

Buy a small supply of good quality loose leaf black tea from the three well-known areas of India: Darjeeling, Assam and Nilgiri. You might purchase these from the same tea vendor or from three different vendors. Experiment with brewing and drinking these teas. Then, in your tea tasting journal, compare the details such as color, aroma and taste of each tea.

Strange how a teapot can represent at the same time the comforts of solitude and the pleasures of company.

Author unknown

CHAPTER 19

Pu-erh Teas

Many years ago, my husband and I traveled to Savannah, Georgia, to stay with friends for a week. We walked along the beach, toured historical houses and relaxed with our books. But our most memorable and delightful time was the afternoon we spent at the Gryphon Tea Room.

This amazing cafe is the epitome of Southern hospitality, elegance and charm. Located in historic Savannah, it offers an exquisite yet traditional afternoon tea service. In the tea-themed gift shop, I purchased a black and gold mug that I still love using for an afternoon tea break.

As part of my tea education, I had recently learned about pu-erh teas and was happy to see the Gryphon had this tea for sale. When I told the clerk I'd like to purchase some pu-erh, she hesitated, then asked me if I was sure. She told me pu-erh tea was an acquired taste and she didn't want me to be disappointed if I didn't like it.

I assured her I was on a mission to explore the world of tea and was willing to take a risk. From that purchase, I discovered the unusual yet satisfying taste of pu-erh tea. With a very mellow, smooth taste, pu-erh tea has become one of my favorites for sharing with friends who are not familiar with this fascinating tea.

Despite the dark color of pu-erh tea, flavors in this category are completely different from dark styles such as black tea. Instead of going through typical tea oxidation, pu-erh tea gets its dark color through a process of microbial fermentation.

To accomplish this, pu-erh tea leaves are lightly roasted before being compressed, where they go through the microbial fermentation process. Over time, this step alters the molecular compounds within the leaf, transforming the taste into a flavor unlike any other style of tea. Many people describe the pu-erh taste as being "of the earth."

Pu-erh tea is typically steeped in a gaiwan tea bowl. The tea is usually brewed gong fu style, in which the leaves are immersed in hot water for only a short time before the tea is poured into another container. The best pu-erh teas can be steeped up to 10-12 times before beginning to lose their flavor.

Often, pu-erh leaves and buds are compressed into individually wrapped cakes marked with information detailing the village or tea factory where they were manufactured. To steep the tea, you simply break off chunks from the tea cake and infuse them with boiling water. You can also find pu-erh sold as loose leaf tea.

As you study this tea, you will find several different spellings for it, including pu-er, puer, pu-erh and pu'erh. In this book I have chosen to refer to the tea as pu-erh.

Remember to review the *Periodic Table of TalkingTea* at the beginning of this book. You'll see pu-erh teas listed in the seventh row.

Here are two of the most known pu-erh teas.

Sheng

Sheng (pronounced like "young") means raw or uncooked. This tea is produced in Yunnan province, China, in a lush, subtropical and mountainous region where many of the tea plants qualify as being ancient because they're more than a hundred years old. This pu-erh tea undergoes a natural post-production fermentation. Living organisms on the surface of the sheng tea leaves, combined with humidity and time, result in mellowing the astringent leaf.

This pu-erh tea is slowly aged or fermented over a long period of time, sometimes 10–50 years. The tea can be drunk young, but it acquires the best flavor after a decade or more of aging. Sheng teas are considered fully mature after aging for 30 years. Sheng tea is often used for digestive properties and cleansing actions. It is also known as a slimming tea.

Shou

Because of the demand for pu-erh, in the 1970s, tea growers developed a new type of pu-erh tea named shou, which means ripe or cooked. Pronounced like "show," shou tea is made in factories using the "wo dui" process of artificially accelerated fermentation.

The tea leaves are spread in a deep pile and dampened with mists of water. Then a thermal blanket is placed over the leaves to bring about a rapid fermentation of 45–70 days. Shou pu-erh tea is meant for immediate consumption, and the flavor improves only slightly with aging.

This pu-erh tea is more reasonably priced than sheng pu-erh, so it might be a good place to start with your pu-erh adventures. Before steeping, rinse the tea in hot water for five seconds to start opening the leaves. Then pour the water off and add fresh hot water for steeping. You can brew numerous short infusions, which will make your tea produce a lot of servings.

EXPLORE

You have come to the last category on the *Periodic Table of TalkingTea*—pu-erh. There is much to explore about this unique fermented tea. You might purchase and try pu-erh tea from two or three vendors so you can compare the size, quality and taste of the teas. You may also want to explore the difference between loose pu-erh tea and pu-erh tea compressed into a tea cake.

And finally, try some samples of sheng (raw or uncooked) and shou (cooked or ripe) pu-erh. With shou pu-erh, the aging process has been accelerated so it's immediately drinkable, while Sheng pu-erh needs to be aged for at least five years, and some have been aged for many years. Generally, the older the pu-erh, the higher the price.

*Although my neighbors are all barbarians, and you, you are a
thousand miles away, there are always two cups on my table.*

– Tang Dynasty (618-906 CE)

CHAPTER 20

Herbal Teas and Tisanes

My family members all know about my love of tea and all things related to it. They are aware that I own close to one hundred teapots. They also know that I have several drawers and shelves in my pantry filled with a wide variety of teas. I never get tired of trying new tea infusions and learning more about the vast subject of tea.

When my son and his wife visited me recently, they described in detail their latest trip to India, where she has family members. They also told many stories about their experiences with tea in that country. But the most fun part of their visit was my young grandson handing me a small white bag.

"Here, Grandma," he said. "We brought you this because we didn't think you have enough tea!" Inside the bag was a fragrant tulsi or "holy basil" tea, which is native to India. I loved the gift, but I also loved his sweet voice teasing me about my supply of tea.

You may not want to have a huge supply of teas, but I encourage you to keep trying new ones as well as learning more about the ones you love.

For many of you, your favorite teas are not teas at all. Only infusions made from the camellia sinensis plant can properly be called teas. So while we call herbal infusions tea, they technically do not match that definition.

Teas made from plants other than the camellia sinensis are considered tisanes, which is the French word for herbal infusions. Because "tea" has become such a familiar term, feel free to still call them that, but keep in mind that they belong to a different category of beverages.

Tisanes can be made from any section of the plant, including the bark, stems, roots, flowers, seeds, leaves and fruit. Over the years, herbal infusions have become known for their healing properties and functional health benefits. In fact, for centuries, tisanes have been an essential component of traditional Chinese medicine and are used for treating many illnesses and health issues.

Some herbal teas are said to detoxify the body and cleanse the liver. Others are promoted for their ability to have a calming effect or anti-inflammatory benefits that help reduce arthritis and joint pain. Many tisanes are used to improve skin, hair and nails, while others ease digestion and other gastrointestinal discomforts.

My grandson's gift of tulsi or holy basil tea has become one of my favorite tisanes. Known for its strong antioxidant properties, this infusion has a sweet flavor and fragrant aroma.

Some of the many health benefits attributed to tulsi include relieving headaches, reducing the effects of colds and flu, boosting concentration and memory and reducing stress. I fell in love with this infusion and have begun using it as a soothing and relaxing drink before bedtime.

Benefits of herbal and decaffeinated teas

While research has focused primarily on traditional tea plants, we know that thousands of tea drinkers have compiled a huge list of benefits from herbal teas.

There's even a trend toward drinking tea for functional benefits, such as better sleep, losing weight and improving energy. Health-conscious tea drinkers now look for botanical blends that include wellness ingredients such as turmeric, ginger, black pepper, rooibos and honey bush.

Here is a short list of reported benefits from the most common herbal teas. This list shows only the most typical tisanes, but you can find dozens of herbal tea varieties as well as descriptions of ways they improve health and well-being.

Chamomile

Chamomile tea soothes and calms people as well as helping them fall asleep faster, making it the perfect bedtime tea. It also has anti-inflammatory properties that may help regulate blood sugar and reduce the severity of menstrual cramps.

Peppermint

This tea is known for soothing discomforts of the digestive tract. The oil that's the basis for peppermint tea can help relieve nausea, cramping, spasms and stomach pain.

Rooibos (pronounced ROY-boss)

In addition to containing antioxidants and anti-inflammatory compounds, rooibos tea has been tied to bone health protection, improved digestive health and obesity prevention.

Ginger

Sipping ginger tea can offer relief from nausea, morning sickness and motion sickness. Ginger root also decreases inflammation, as in lessening muscle discomfort after intense exercise and reducing pain in people with osteoarthritis.

Rose hips

Rose hip tea is high in vitamin C and antioxidants. Its anti-inflammatory properties may reduce inflammation and pain associated with arthritis. Studies have also found rose hips effective at fighting aging of the skin and reducing stomach fat.

Lemon

Lemon balm tea appears to reduce cortisol, a stress hormone, so it can help you feel calmer and more relaxed. Because it doesn't cause drowsiness, it provides a great choice for helping you get through a difficult work day.

Lavender

Many people find drinking lavender tea at bedtime helps them sleep better as well as feel more rested the next day.

Where to find herbal teas

Many supermarkets now stock a wide variety of herbal teas and tisanes in the tea and coffee aisle or the health food section. You will also find many wonderful varieties at health food stores and specialty shops. In some locations, you can even mix a combination of teas to make your own personal infusion.

You might like to experiment with making tisanes by growing your own herbs or purchasing specific herbs, stems and flowers. Once you have your combination of ingredients, boil them in a large container of water to help release their flavors, nutrients and health properties. Plan to use a stainless steel pot for this because aluminum, iron and copper containers will affect the ingredients as well as the taste.

Be sure to check with your doctor before ingesting large amounts of herbal infusions to make sure they don't interfere with your medications or cause any allergic reactions. With children, it's fine to use caffeine-free tisanes as a fun way to introduce them to the health and social benefits of these beverages.

EXPLORE

You are probably familiar with many common herbal teas, such as chamomile and peppermint. But in your goal of increasing your knowledge of tea, experiment with some of the more unusual ones. Try lavender or ginger tea and notice any specific benefits from them. Taste new tisanes such as rose hips or lemon balm.

Pay attention to any specific benefits you notice from your herbal teas. For example, do they calm you down, help you sleep or perhaps improve your concentration and ability to focus? Make notes in your tea tasting journal about which ones help you the most. Then be sure to always maintain a good supply of those special tisanes.

I expect I shall feel better after tea.

– P.G. Wodehouse, author of *Carry on Jeeves* (1881-1975)

CHAPTER 21

Fun and Functional Teas

Have you been feeling tired or run down? Do you have trouble with digestion or other body functions? Maybe you are trying to lose weight, build stronger muscles or improve joint health. It must be time for a cup of tea.

In response to consumer demands for natural health remedies, many tea companies have begun adding a variety of products such as vitamins and herbs to their popular teas. This has led to an entirely new category called "functional teas," which offer potential solutions to many areas of health and wellness.

Even though most of the health claims aren't supported by scientific evidence, functional teas have become extremely popular, and new versions keep showing up. Recently, companies have even created teas with added probiotics and encourage you to drink those teas for digestive health.

As you explore some of these fun and functional teas, be sure to check with your physician about any contraindications based on your health conditions or medications.

Tea Extracts

A tea extract is made by evaporating the liquid used for steeping tea leaves and creating a dry, concentrated form of the tea. Some tea extracts contain added caffeine, antioxidants and flavonoids or other ingredients with possible health benefits. You can find tea extracts in a variety of strengths and types including tablets, capsules, pills, liquids and powders.

To make powdered extracts, tea leaves are soaked in alcohol or another solution to infuse the active ingredients. The liquid is then reduced and concentrated and finally dehydrated into powdered form.

Tea extracts offer the benefits of a beverage such as green tea without you having to drink five or six cups per day. Instead, you can swallow a capsule or add a powdered extract to a smoothie. Compared to brewed tea, some extracts contain higher levels of caffeine, so be careful if you are caffeine-sensitive. And since concentrated tea extracts may change the effects of medications, you may want to discuss the use of them with your doctor.

Vegetable Teas

Is it soup or is it tea? Some companies are experimenting with teas made to taste like a salad or fresh produce from your garden. You can find teas made from broccoli, beetroot, carrots, kale and other vegetables. Most of these teas can be brewed hot or cold as well as added to juices or smoothies, which give bright, vivid colors to your drink.

Kombucha or Mushroom Tea

A fermented tonic drink, kombucha is made from a base of strong black or green sweetened tea. There are many health claims and healing powers attributed to kombucha, such as activating metabolism and enhancing performance of mind and body. Kombucha is sold in many grocery or specialty stores as a ready-to-drink beverage.

Making kombucha at home requires a starter fungus called a "mushroom," which is a colony of bacteria and yeast. Along with a starter solution, this mushroom is added to freshly brewed and cooled sweetened tea. The tea is set in a warm place to ferment for one to two weeks, then bottled and stored for a couple of weeks to encourage carbonation. After that, the bottled kombucha is put into a refrigerated environment to slow down the process of carbonation and fermentation.

Scientists caution about the potential contamination and harmful bacteria when kombucha is made at home, so be sure to follow strict guidelines if you try this.

Because some people have allergic reactions to kombucha, it's best to taste only a tablespoonful at first and check your response. If you are fine, you can gradually increase the amount, up to a few ounces two or three times a day, until you are confident you can handle kombucha.

Rooibos

The rooibos herb comes from the needle-like leaves of the bush *aspalathus linearis*, which is native to South Africa. You may see it also called rooibosch, which is the Dutch word for "red tea." The herbal tea processed from the rooibos bush has a natural sweetness and is caffeine-free. It's also full of antioxidants and is said to decrease insomnia, aid digestion and relieve cold and flu symptoms. Rooibos blends well with fruits, spices and other flavors and makes a delicious iced tea.

Yerba Mate

An evergreen shrub grown mostly in Brazil, Argentina, Paraguay and Uruguay, yerba mate (*ilex paraguariensis*) is high in caffeine and is said to improve mental energy. Traditionally, the leaves of yerba mate are infused in a hollow gourd called a guampa and sipped through a bombilla, which is a metal straw.

To make yerba mate tea, the dried leaves are placed in the gourd and infused with hot, not boiling, water. If lightly brewed, the infusion tastes a little like green tea. But if it's brewed longer, the tea may taste a bit like tobacco. The leaves can usually be steeped twice.

High in antioxidants, yerba mate may be slightly diuretic and is said to dampen hunger pangs. You can usually find yerba mate tea bags in grocery or specialty stores. Often the teas will have added flavorings such as lemon, bergamot, cinnamon or mint.

Moringa

Moringa is a plant native to India, Pakistan, Bangladesh and Afghanistan. In these countries, every part of moringa is used as a food source, mostly because the plant can be grown so cheaply.

The immature green pods (drumsticks) are prepared similarly to green beans. With more mature pods, the seeds are removed and cooked or roasted. The leaves of the plant can be cooked and used similar to spinach, but they can also be dried and powdered for use as a condiment.

As an antioxidant, moringa is said to be helpful in treating asthma, diabetes, obesity, menopause and other conditions. Of course, as with many herbal plants, there is no scientific evidence yet to support these claims.

Ashwagandha

Native to India, ashwagandha is a short, perennial shrub whose Latin name (*withania somnifera*) translates to "sleep-inducing."

Ashwagandha is a known adaptogen, meaning it improves the body's ability to manage mental, physical and emotional stress. It has a bold, earthy flavor, so some people like to add spices, milk or a bit of sweetener, such as honey or maple syrup. This tea is a staple of Ayurveda, the popular Indian alternative medicine and healing system.

Maca

Sometimes referred to as Peruvian ginseng, maca is a plant that grows in central Peru in the high plateaus of the Andes Mountains. A relative of the radish, maca has been cultivated as a vegetable crop in this area for at least 3000 years. In the Andes, maca root is used medicinally for treating anemia, infertility, sexual dysfunction and other conditions.

Generally, the maca root is dried and consumed in powdered form, but it's also available in capsules and as a liquid extract. The taste of maca root powder has been described as earthy and nutty. Some people mask the taste by adding it to smoothies or other foods.

Purple Tea

Purple tea is a rare tea variety developed and grown in Kenya. It requires cooler conditions and grows best at a high elevation of 3500 to 7500 feet, which allows the plant to absorb intense sun rays.

The purple appearance of the tea is caused by a unique genetic mutation which produces anthocyanin, the same antioxidant found in blueberries. Purple tea also has high levels of catechins, especially EGCG, which is the powerful ingredient found in green tea.

Masala Chai

Although masala chai is actually a black tea, I've included it here because it contains several spices that make it a unique beverage. *Chai* is the Hindi word for "tea" and *masala* is the Hindi word for "spice," so loosely translated masala chai means "spice tea." Keep in mind that since the word chai means tea, if you say "chai tea," you are actually saying "tea tea."

In India, street or roadside tea vendors, called chai wallahs, add a variety of spices, milk and sweeteners to strong Assam black tea to make masala chai. Typical spices include cloves, star anise, cinnamon, cardamom, black pepper and nutmeg. Chai sold in stores and restaurants in the U.S. usually contains ginger as well as spices similar to the ones in Indian chai.

Bubble Tea

In the late 1980s, people in Taiwan invented a tea-based drink they called bubble tea. Originally a black tea with large, chewy black tapioca balls, bubble tea is now available in many flavors and in concentrated sweet syrups. Also known as boba tea or pearl tea, this fun drink has become especially popular with millennials and can be found on the menus of many coffee shops and restaurants.

To make the tea, large dried tapioca pearls are cooked about 15 minutes, sweetened with a syrup, then cooled. The tapioca is ladled into a cup or glass filled with strongly brewed tea and then topped with milk or fruit juice. The tapioca floats from the top to the bottom of the drink and you can suck the squishy, sweet tapioca up through a fat straw, allowing you to both "eat and drink" the bubble tea.

Cheese Tea

One of the latest trends from Asia is cheese tea. This drink is made with cold green or black tea topped with a foamy layer of milk and cream cheese, then sprinkled with a pinch of salt and sugar. This tea originated in Taiwan in 2010 and is especially popular in Hong Kong, Singapore and Malaysia. The taste of this rich and creamy tea is sweet, like bubble tea, but with a savory finish.

EXPLORE

Purchase a good quality loose leaf Assam black tea and experiment with adding spices to make your own masala chai. You can find easy recipes and suggestions for this online. Try several combinations and varying amounts to see which ones you like best. Note how your version compares with chai you purchase in a store or at a tea or coffee shop.

Resources

Caffeine Levels Chart

In Chapter 6, you read about the caffeine levels in the main varieties of tea and how they compare to the amount of caffeine in coffee.

For an easy comparison, here is a chart that shows the approximate caffeine content per 8-ounce cup:

Type of tea	Caffeine content
Herbal and rooibos	0 mg
Decaf tea	2–6 mg
White tea	10–15 mg
Green tea	15–30 mg
Oolong tea	30–45 mg
Black tea	60–75 mg
Matcha tea	60–80 mg
Yerba mate tea	70–85 mg
Coffee	125–150 mg

You can't get a cup of tea large enough
or a book long enough to suit me.
– C.S. Lewis, British author (1898-1963)

My 20 Favorite Tea Books

Many years ago, I purchased *The Republic of Tea*, the story of how a unique specialty tea company was born. Already a passionate tea drinker, I was excited to learn more about specialty teas and the advantages of drinking high-grade loose leaf tea.

Soon my curiosity led me to purchase more books on tea as well as study the tea industry and attend tea conferences. Now I own nearly 350 books on tea and, far from considering myself an expert, I feel there is so much more to learn.

In this section, I have listed some of my all-time favorite books on tea. They are all available from Amazon and other online book vendors.

I encourage you to choose one or two books that sound interesting and take your study of tea even deeper. Eventually you might even create your own tea book library.

By the way, if you like cozy murder mysteries, you'll enjoy the Tea Shop Mystery books by Laura Childs. There are now 20 books in the series with each book including recipes and tips for serving tea. They are fun to read while you continue to learn more about tea.

Here are my twenty favorite tea books, divided into helpful categories.

Practical guides for beginners

Tea Basics: A Quick and Easy Guide by Wendy Rasmussen and
Ric Rhinehart. Houghton Mifflin Harcourt, 1998
This handy reference covers all the essentials of tea
buying, brewing and tasting. In addition, you'll learn about
the origin, history and varieties of several teas along with tips
on tea etiquette. The authors help you explore the history of
the Japanese tea ceremony as well as afternoon tea. They also
examine the scientific studies on tea and include details on the
amount of caffeine in different teas.

*The Tea Enthusiast's Handbook: A Guide to Enjoying the
World's Best Teas* by Mary Lou Heiss and Robert J. Heiss. Ten
Speed Press, 2010
This book provides an authoritative guide to understanding
tea and its origins. It includes the many ways to buy tea, how
to explore and enjoy the six types of tea, and how to properly
steep a perfect cup of tea. It includes photos and tasting notes
for more than 35 teas, information on the grades of tea, and a
helpful glossary.

The Harney & Sons Guide to Tea by Michael Harney. Penguin
Press, 2008
Written by one of the country's leading tea professionals,
this guide profiles tea varieties from delicate white to aged pu-
erh, revealing how each tea is distinctive. The author explains
how the taste of each tea is influenced by a combination of
cultivation and production techniques as well as geography. He
also recommends a proper brewing temperature and appropriate
brewing time for each tea variety.

Green Tea: A Quest for Fresh Leaf and Timeless Craft by Hugo
America and others. Benjamin Press, 2015
Four tea professionals from Canada developed the well-
known "Camellia Sinensis Tea Houses" in Montreal and Quebec

City. Each year they travel the world in search of outstanding teas. Color photos and lovely water color paintings illustrate this book devoted to artisanal green teas. The authors give you steeping notes and suggested techniques for making a great cup of green tea.

A Little Tea Book: All the Essentials from Leaf to Cup by Sebastian Beckwith, Caroline Paul and Wendy MacNaughton. Bloomsbury Publishing, 2018

Each chapter of this book starts with "A little on..." and includes content on a variety of tea-related topics. There's a little on the tea plant, the six types of tea, choosing tea, tea labels, tea and health, etc. You'll be delighted by the watercolors of various tea shapes, information on how to select teas by flavor, and tips on how to get the correct water temperature without using a thermometer. The book includes an extensive glossary along with additional recommended readings.

Fun tea books

Infused: Adventures in Tea by Henrietta Lovell. Faber and Faber, 2019

Henrietta Lovell, the owner of Rare Tea Company, travels the world to discover rare and precious teas and her company purchases tea directly from individual tea growers. This intrepid woman's quest for extraordinary teas has taken her from Malawi to the Himalayas, from Wuyi Shan in China to Mexico. Part travel writing, part memoir, Lovell includes photographs and recipes from her travels and her work with renowned hotels and restaurants.

The Agony of the Leaves: The Ecstasy of My Life with Tea by Helen Gustafson. Henry Holt and Company, 1996

The famed tea guru of Berkeley's Chez Panisse restaurant, Gustafson delighted us with her descriptions of the domestic tea rituals of her St. Paul, Minnesota upbringing, including the recipe for her surprisingly tasty "pepper toast." Her storytelling, recipes and the description of her first meeting with Mr. Twining, of the Twining tea empire, make this a delightful book you will want to read again and again.

The Republic of Tea: The Story of the Creation of a Business as Told Through the Personal Letters of Its Founders by Mel Ziegler, Patricia Ziegler, Bill Rosenzweig. Crown Business, 1994

Correspondence between Mel and Patricia Ziegler, founders of The Banana Republic, and their new tea business partner, Bill Rosenzweig, gives entrepreneurs an inside view of how a revolutionary tea company came to be. This book guides the reader through the creative process and includes a user's guide to help readers use the book's practical ideas.

History and origin of tea

Tea at the Blue Lantern Inn: A Social History of the Tea Room Craze in America by Jan Whitaker. St. Martin's Press, 2002

At the turn of the last century, many tea rooms, often owned and operated by women, popped up across America. Sparked by the suffragist movement, prohibition and the rise of the automobile industry, tea rooms started a trend of small restaurants and coffee bars. From roadside tea rooms to high-society tea restaurants at posh city hotels, Whitaker chronicles the social, artistic and culinary changes brought about by tea rooms. This look at America's past includes vintage photos and illustrations.

The Classic of Tea: Origins and Rituals by Lu Yu. Ecco Press, 1995

Written during the eighth century's Tang Dynasty, Lu Yu's book provides tea drinkers with practical and spiritual knowledge of the art of tea brewing. Translated and introduced years later by Francis Ross Carpenter, this was the first complete translation of the book to appear in the Western World. It includes several beautiful black and white illustrations.

Tea: History, Terroirs, Varieties by Kevin Gascoyne and others. Firefly Books, 2018

A comprehensive guide to tea that includes many color photographs, this book will take you on a tour of the world's tea growing countries: China, Japan, Taiwan, India, Sri Lanka, Nepal, Vietnam and East Africa. It includes an overview of the history of tea, how tea is processed, tea varieties, signature tea cultivars, as well as the art of making, serving and tasting tea. The book includes 15 tea recipes from gourmet chefs and a directory of teas. The detailed charts, tables and graphs provide information on the caffeine, antioxidant and other biochemical properties of 35 different teas.

The Book of Tea by Kakuzo Okakura. Benjamin Press, 2019

In the early 20th century, Okakura lived in Boston, where he was the Director of the Asian Arts Department at the Museum of Fine Arts. Originally published in 1906, his "philosophy of beauty and tranquility" introduced the art of tea to Americans. He was also the spiritual advisor for Isabella Stewart Gardner, a "grande dame" in the wealthy Back Bay society of Boston.

A Social History of Tea: Tea's Influence on Commerce, Culture and Community by Jane Pettigrew and Bruce Richardson. Benjamin Press, 2013

British writer and tea historian, Jane Pettigrew, and American tea writer, Bruce Richardson, chronicle the story of tea's influence on British and American culture over nearly four centuries. This is a fascinating story of how the leaves of the Asian plant, camellia sinensis, shaped the culture and politics of the United Kingdom and the United States.

Learning and reference books

The New Tea Companion: A Guide to Teas Throughout the World by Jane Pettigrew and Bruce Richardson. Benjamin Press, 2015

This book offers descriptions and images of the character, taste and appearance of more than one hundred teas from China, India, Sri Lanka, Kenya, Japan, Taiwan and Indonesia. Well-known and respected tea experts, the authors guide readers toward some of the best teas and share details on tea cultures and tea ceremonies.

Tea Sommelier: A Step-by-Step Guide by Francois-Xavier Delmas and Mathias Minet. Abbeville Press Publishers, 2016

From the founders of the international tea brand, "Palais des Thés," this book provides a fun and simple approach to becoming a tea expert. Every page is a self-contained lesson with stylish illustrations. The topics include different varieties of tea and where they are grown, how to select and prepare tea, how to taste and serve it, how to pair tea with food and how to cook with tea. It gives you knowledge and practical tips on tea in 160 easy lessons.

The Tea Book: Experience the World's Finest Teas, Qualities, Infusions, Rituals, Recipes by Linda Gaylard. DK (Penguin Random House), 2015

In this book, the author explores tea plantations in the world's most important growing regions from India to Kenya. She covers tea blends, tastings and ceremonies from around the world along with tips for steeping each variety of tea. She suggests participating in a tasting course to cultivate your sense of tea color, aroma and taste. The book also includes 75 classic and contemporary recipes.

World Atlas of Tea: From the Leaf to the Cup, the World's Teas Explored and Enjoyed by Krisi Smith. Firefly Books, 2016

In this book, the author follows tea from the plantation to harvesting to processing to making the perfect cup of tea. The book covers tea basics, tea brewing and drinking, and tea blending. The author also describes the world of tea through country profiles of China, Taiwan, Japan, India, Nepal, Sri Lanka, Vietnam and East Africa. The book includes many color photographs.

The Story of Tea: A Cultural History and Drinking Guide by Mary Lou Heiss and Robert J. Heiss. Ten Speed Press, 2007

A sweeping tour through the world of tea, this book provides a complete reference for choosing, drinking and enjoying tea. The authors profile more than thirty essential tea varietals as well as survey the customs and crafts associated with tea. This well-illustrated book concludes with ten sweet and savory recipes made with tea and includes resources for purchasing tea.

Tea: A User's Guide by Tony Gebely. Eggs and Toast Media LLC, 2016

This factual guide to specialty teas describes how tea is grown and processed and the chemical changes that occur in tea leaves during processing. It also tells how 130 famous teas from around the world are classified as well as how to expertly prepare and evaluate tea.

James Norwood Pratt's Tea Dictionary by James Norwood Pratt. Tea Society, 2010

A handbook for the international tea trade, this book is a great resource for all tea lovers. It provides details on all principal kinds of tea grown in the world, along with a timeline of tea history, maps and striking photography. It also includes detailed descriptions of many teas and tea gardens. The author of several books on tea, Pratt has covered the tea industry for over 30 years and is America's acknowledged "Tea Sage."

Detailed Listing of 48 Special Teas

As you continue your journey to becoming a tea connoisseur, I encourage you to dig deeper into the history and background of many different types of tea.

The tea listings in this section will give you a starting place for learning more about the many categories of tea as well as the types and flavors of specific ones. You'll also learn where the teas are grown as well as interesting facts about how they are harvested and produced for the tea market.

Explore a new tea

As you read through the tea lists, consider trying a new tea at intervals, such as weekly or monthly. Choose a specific one from the most common teas in a category, such as green or black tea, and spend some time learning about your selected tea.

Deepen your knowledge of where that type of tea is grown, the way the tea is harvested and how it is processed. As you sip a cup of your new tea, picture a detailed landscape including the field of tea plants and the workers who cultivate and harvest the tea leaves. Then imagine those same people relaxing with a cup of tea after a hard day at work.

You might add to your knowledge by researching your new tea online, looking for stories and legends around that specific type of tea. Find pictures showing details of the tea leaves, buds and stalks of your tea. Study how you could recognize that tea by sight, aroma and taste.

Be sure to record details about it in your Tea Tasting Journal so you can refer to your notes when you want to taste it again.

As you experiment with each new type of tea, I strongly suggest you purchase only loose leaf teas.

48 Special Teas

This section will help you learn the background and details about 48 special teas that are the most loved in the tea world. I haven't tried all of these teas and, in fact, some of them are difficult to find. But one of my goals is to buy a small sample of all 48 and do a systematic tasting.

In the listings for each individual tea, note that the steeping temperatures and times are simply recommendations. Feel free to experiment and determine your own personal preferences.

The tea names in this list are grouped into the six general categories:

◇ White Teas
◇ Yellow Teas
◇ Green Teas
◇ Oolong Teas
◇ Black Teas
◇ Pu-erh Teas

The list follows the exact order the teas appear in the *Periodic Table of TalkingTea* at the beginning of this book.

WHITE TEAS

White Tip Silver Needle
Bai Hao Yin Zhen

From: Fujian Province in China

Appearance: This tea has an air-dried white leaf that looks like silver needles; the leaf with unopened new buds is covered in silver-white hairs.

Harvested: Usually picked by hand on two days a year in the spring, between March 15 and April 10

Processed: This tea is withered and slowly air-dried to about 5% oxidation, sometimes with a bake-drying as well.

Details: The original white tea, first produced in 1885, is now considered one of China's Ten Most Famous Teas. Known as the highest grade of white tea, there is a small amount of production, making this tea the most expensive of traditional bud style white teas.

Steeping: 160-170°F, 2 to 3 minutes

Liquor: Pale silver color or light amber yellow

Aroma: Clean, floral, sweet, sometimes the aroma of apricot or artichoke

Flavor: Smooth, sweet, silky, soft, sometimes vegetal, with taste of fresh apricots, peaches, honey or artichoke

White Peony
Bai Mu Dan

From: Fujian Province in China

Appearance: This rare tea has very small buds covered in silvery down.

Harvested: Plucked in early spring, usually including one shoot and two open leaves

Processed: Air-dried, naturally dried indoors or machine-dried at low temperatures to 5-12 % oxidation

Details: First produced in 1922 from the leaves of Fuding DaBai or Zhenghe DaBai tea bushes, this tea is less expensive than

Yin Zhen and has a more intense flavor. The more tips, the better the tea.

Steeping: 160-170°F, 2 to 3 minutes

Liquor: Clear, pale orange-yellow liquor with a pale straw to light amber color, or yellow-green

Aroma: Clean, fresh aroma with notes of clean clay, honeyed, lightly vegetal

Flavor: Smooth, soft, delicate, sweet, slight earthiness or woodiness

Long Life Eyebrow or Longevity Eyebrow
Shou Mei, Sow Mei or Shu Mee

From: Fujian Province in China

Appearance: The leaf is not all one color, but a mix of shades – light green, greenish light gray.

Harvested: Coarser in leaf quality and darker in color and fuller in body, this tea is plucked later in the season. The pluck is a grouping of 3-4 large leaves.

Processed: Naturally withered in the sun or naturally dried indoors to 5-12 % oxidation

Details: Shou Mei is a lower grade white tea, made from different varietals. Since the days of the Song Dynasty, white tea has been produced in Fujian Province, China. Now, a small amount of white tea is produced in Anhui Province and in Assam, Darjeeling, Nilgiri and Sri Lanka.

Steeping: 175-195°F, 1 to 2 minutes, steep less time in a gaiwan

Liquor: Darker in color than Bai Mu Dan, pale yellow

Aroma: Sweet, floral aroma

Flavor: Like some lighter oolong teas, fruit-like

Tribute Eyebrow
Gong Mei

From: Fujian Province in China

Appearance: This tea consists of broken leaf and a few buds and can be made from many varietals.

Harvested: Picked after the production of Bai Hao Yin Zhen and Bai Mu Dan is completed

Processed: More quickly processed than Bai Hao Yin Zhen or Bai Mu Dan.

Details: This lowest grade of white tea from Fujian Province is called Tribute Eyebrow because of the delicately curved eyebrow shape. It can be made from many varietals, from only the large leaves of the Xiao Bai tea bush cultivar or from brown broken leaves with a few buds. This common white tea is often found in Southern Chinese restaurants.

Steeping: 185°F, 2 minutes – can do multiple infusions

Liquor: Pale, almost white

Aroma: Apples

Flavor: Light sweetness, fruity flavor, very clean taste

YELLOW TEAS

Jun Shan Silver Needle
Jun Shan Yin Zhen

From: Junshan Island in Hunan Province's Dong Ting Lake

Appearance: The needle-like leaf is pointed on both ends and rises and falls repeatedly while steeping.

Harvested: Once a year around April 20

Processed: Small batches of tea leaves are wrapped in cloth bundles after fixing, allowing them to turn from green to yellow-green.

Details: This rare yellow tea has more depth than Yin Zhen white tea and is generally expensive due to limited production. It is the only yellow tea among China's Ten Most Famous Teas.

Steeping: 170-185°F, 3 to 5 minutes

Liquor: Pale yellow, golden

Aroma: Fresh, reminiscent of flowers and nuts or tropical fruit

Flavor: Chestnut and hazelnut, creaminess

Yellow Sprouting
Huo Shan Huang Ya

From: This prized yellow tea is from the Huo Shan area of Anhui Province in China.

Appearance: Long slender leaves, twisted-needle bud set

Harvested: The pluck is a bud and one leaf with a twisted needle bud set.

Processed: The tea leaves are pan-fired, sometimes wrapped in small bundles, and then dried. The production process blocks enzymes that cause oxidation and cause young shoots to turn yellow.

Details: This yellow tea is sometimes called a green tea, but is sold in the West as a yellow tea. It was first produced in the Tang Dynasty and offered as a Tribute Tea to the Imperial Court during the Ming and Qing Dynasties. High in antioxidants, this ancient tea's production method was lost, but production was resumed in 1971.

Steeping: 170-175°F, 2 to 3 minutes

Liquor: Clear straw color, golden yellow, resembles a green oolong

Aroma: Softly herbaceous like "sweet grass," aroma of nuts (chestnuts, hazelnuts), floral fragrance, ginger

Flavor: Smoothness, "waxiness," sweet after taste, rounded, mellow, refreshing

Yellow Sprout
Meng Ding Huang Ya

From: Northwestern Sichuan Province in China

Appearance: The buds are short and tender

Harvested: An early bud set is plucked.

Processed: This tea undergoes a step called men huan or "sealing yellow" – the tea is lightly steamed, then covered with a cloth to allow the leaves to breathe.

Details: This very rare yellow tea was first produced in the Han Dynasty about 2000 years ago and was selected as an Imperial Tea in the Tang Dynasty. Meng Ding Huang Ya tea is rarely found outside China because limited quantities are produced.

Steeping: 170-180°F, 2 to 3 minutes – can infuse several times

Liquor: Clear, pale straw color with tinge of pale green, pale yellow

Aroma: Clean, some scent of freshly mown hay

Flavor: Slightly toasty, sweet, brisk, smooth notes of hazelnuts and chestnuts

Yellow Buds

Mo Gan Huang Ya

From: Mo Gan Shan area of eastern Zhejiang Province in China

Appearance: Leaves are slightly yellow, shiny or waxy

Harvested: One bud and one leaf are picked later than most spring teas, usually around April 20th.

Processed: Slightly oxidized

Details: Production of this yellow tea dates back 1000 years to the Song Dynasty. Production was stopped for a time and only resumed in 1979. It's the hardest of the yellow teas to find in the West.

Steeping: 185°F, 2 minutes – as many as six infusions

Liquor: Bright, slightly yellow color, yellowish-green

Aroma: Fresh apricots, crispy rice

Flavor: Subtle, rich, tropical fruit note, floral to nutty, lingering aftertaste

 GREEN TEAS

Green Snail Spring or Green Spring Spiral
Bi Lo Chun, Bi Luo Chun or Pi Lo Chun

From: Jiangsu Province in China

Appearance: The leaf looks like downy fluff, because the small, dark green, spiraled leaves are coated in fuzzy yellow down.

Harvested: One leaf and the bud is picked. Bi Lo Chun is produced in limited quantities during the spring harvest at the end of March.

Processed: The leaves and buds are rolled by hand to form tiny spirals, then hot-air fired.

Details: One of China's Ten Most Famous Teas, this rare tea has a snail-like appearance.

Steeping: Slightly cooler than 175-185°F, 2 to 3 minutes

Because of the leaf's delicacy, water for steeping should be cooler than 175°F, ideal for other greens. Add the leaf to water, rather than pouring water on the leaves or the tea quickly develops an astringency.

Liquor: Clear golden or pale green, velvety or thick

Aroma: Light, sweet, faintly citrusy, floral (orange)

Flavor: Clean, fresh, slightly sweet, faint hint of jasmine

Dragonwell
Long Jing, Long Jin or Lung Ching

From: Originally from West Lake in Zhejiang Province in China, now produced in Fujian Province in China

Appearance: The narrow, flat green leaves have a jade green color.

Harvested: Picked early spring, mid-March to early April

Processed: The leaves are pan-fired.

Details: There are 8 grades of Long Jing, each with distinctive leaf appearance and varying degrees of flavor, depending on the quantity of buds and leaves. Long Jing was mentioned in the first book dedicated to tea, *The Classic of Tea*, by Lu Yu, which dates to the Tang Dynasty in approximately 760 CE. One of China's Ten Famous Tribute Teas, this tea was formerly enjoyed by only the Emperor during the Qing Dynasty. The tea was praised for having four unique characteristics: jade color, vegetative aroma, mellow chestnut-like flavor and singular shape.

Steeping: 170-180°F, 2 to 3 minutes

Liquor: Brilliant golden yellow, clear yellow, straw-colored, almost amber

Aroma: Nutty, chestnut-like, boiled chestnuts, steamed bok choy

Flavor: Mellow, slightly sweet aftertaste; soft, rich, toasty, yeasty; boiled or roasted chestnut, toasted nuts, vanilla

Hair Points
Mao Jian

From: The misty mountains of Zhejiang, Anhui and Henan Provinces, China

Appearance: The tea has curly, dark seaweed-green leaves with silvery buds and long, neat twists.

Harvested: Picked spring and fall, best quality leaves harvested early to mid-April

Processed: An exceptional spring tea produced in small quantities and partially hand-made

Details: Famous Mao Jians include: Xinyang Mao Jian, Duyun Mao Jian, Jiu King Mao Jian, Guzhang and Weishan Maojian.

Steeping: 160°F, 3 minutes

Liquor: Vivid, pale lime-green, velvety, full-bodied

Aroma: Complex aroma; brisk, clean taste; bright, fresh, clean character that is refreshing

Flavor: Dry grass in back notes and sweeter floral notes in the foreground

Monkey King
Tai Ping Hou Kui

From: Grows on the north slope of one of the Huang Shan mountains in Anhui Province in China

Appearance: Large, bright-green flattened leaves grow between 3 to 6 inches long. The straight, heavy leaf is pointed at both ends.

Harvested: This tea is plucked in late April

Processed: Pan-fired or basket-fired and blotted in between rice paper

Details: One of the Ten Famous Teas of China; first produced in the early 1900s

Steeping: 170-180°F, 2 to 3 minutes – can infuse multiple times

Liquor: Deep straw color or pale light green

Aroma: Toasty, moss-like, vegetal undertones of green beans, floral

Flavor: Earthy, rich, vegetal, delicate sweet taste reminiscent of orchids or toasted zucchini

Heavenly Blue Peaks
Tian Mu Shan (Qing Ding)

From: Tian Mu Shan Mountain which is sometimes called Clouds and Mist, in the Zhejiang Province in China

Appearance: The leaf is tight and dark green strips have visible hair and many leaf-bud sets.

Harvested: Brief period in spring, mid-late April

Processed: One bud and 1-2 tender leaves, evenly shaped, long strips

Details: Tian Mu Shan is one of the famous "Tribute Teas" and is known since the Tang Dynasty. It comes from the cloud and mist zone between 1600-4000 feet in China's Golden Triangle of Tea: Anhui, Zhejiang and Jiangxi Provinces.

Steeping: 185°F, 1 to 2 minutes

Liquor: Bright green or clear yellow

Aroma: Clean aroma of green tea
Flavor: Fresh, clean taste, naturally sweet

Lucky Dragon
Hyson

From: Anhui Province, China
Appearance: Small, curly green leaf called Chun Mee (Precious Eyebrows)
Harvested: This tea is made from young leaves gathered in the early spring before the first rains. The first tea plucked in the spring is the finest.
Processed: The leaves are twisted into long, thin strips.
Details: Young Hyson, considered superior to Hyson, is the trade name for a category of China green tea which varies in quality from poor to almost fine, depending on the origin and time of year of the pluck. Hyson and Young Hyson are terms no longer used in China, where these teas are known as Chun Mee, but are still sometimes called Hyson outside of China.
Steeping: 160-175°F, 3 to 5 minutes
Liquor: Golden-yellow
Aroma: Earthy
Flavor: Smooth, robust flavor and a slightly dry aftertaste; some special Chun Mee or Young Hyson may have a plum-like flavor.

Gunpowder, Pearl Tea or Imperial Pinhead
Zhu Cha

From: Pingshui in Zhejiang Province in China
Appearance: This green tea is in tightly rolled balls of tea resembling gunpowder.
Harvested: Tougher and less tender later season leaves
Processed: Manufactured by tumble firing
Details: The gray-green, rolled leaf pellets are produced almost entirely for export. Generally considered an inexpensive tea,

the smaller the pellets, the more expensive the tea. Zhu Cha is one of the best known and most liked green teas.

Steeping: 175-185°F, 3 to 4 minutes. Tolerates a range of water temperatures and infuses slowly

Liquor: Strong, greenish-coppery liquor or straw color; bright yellow to light brown to green

Aroma: Robust, flinty, burnt wood, slightly nutty

Flavor: Pungent, hearty, robust but sweet, barely vegetal flavor

Sencha

From: 40% of Sencha is grown in Japan's Shizuoka prefecture, the largest tea growing area in Japan.

Appearance: The glossy, 1" leaves are fairly uniform in size.

Harvested: The first harvest in April is considered the best and called Shincha or "new tea." Each flush yields tea of lesser quality and price.

Processed: The flat leaf is steamed and oven-fired, and there is a wide variety of qualities, grades and prices.

Details: Sencha is Japan's most popular tea. The most common grade of Sencha constitutes 80% of Japan's total tea production. The finest is the first flush or "ichiban-cha" or number one tea; 2nd plucking is nibancha; 3rd plucking is sanbancha; 4th plucking is yobancha. Sencha is usually sipped from small cups with savory snacks— never with sweets. Fukamushi Sencha is deeply steamed and is sweeter, richer and less astringent. The Sencha tea ceremony, a simpler style than the formal nature of the Chanoyu powdered tea ceremony, became popular in Japan's Edo period (1603–1868). Loose leaf tea is steeped in a kyusu teapot, a small teapot with the handle attached to and protruding from the side of the teapot.

Steeping: 160-170°F, 2 minutes or 175°F, 1 to 2 minutes. A "fussy" tea, don't steep too hot.

Liquor: Light, artichoke color, clear, sparkling or a vivid, forest green color; rich in amino acids and Vitamin C

Aroma: fresh, green, grass scent, vibrant, grassy and bright, spinachy

Flavor: Only slightly astringent, robust, vegetal; delicate sweetness, delicately herbaceous; rich in amino acids and Vitamin C

Bancha

From: Shizuoka prefecture in Japan

Appearance: Large, hard leaves, including stems

Harvested: After Sencha is plucked, Bancha, a lower market grade, is harvested from the same bushes. The coarse leaf is picked from late summer to fall.

Processsed: Steamed for 15-30 seconds, then rolled or fired

Details: Bancha is a common green Japanese tea. High grade Bancha with less astringency is called Senryu.

Steeping: 175 to 200°F, 30 seconds to 2½ minutes

Liquor: Yellow-green or bright yellow

Aroma: Less fragrant than Sencha

Flavor: Stronger flavor, herbal, spinach, celery, more astringent and grassier than Sencha

Houjicha or Hojicha

From: Shizuoka prefecture in Japan

Appearance: The tea sometimes has no leaves, just light brown wooden stalks.

Harvested: Houjicha is a Bancha with large leaves picked at the end of the harvest or in autumn.

Processed: Usually made by roasting Sencha leaf and Kukicha twig leaf to create a tea with a toasty flavor

Details: This Japanese green tea was discovered in 1920 by a Kyoto merchant. He roasted old Bancha and created a new tea with a new flavor. The tea has relatively little caffeine and tannin and is sometimes served to Japanese children because it's low in caffeine.

Steeping: 175-185°F, 30 seconds, up to 2 to 3 minutes

Liquor: Light-brown to nearly black liquor with shades of gold, caramel brown

Aroma: Fruity, woody, hint of spiciness, nutty fragrance, roasted coffee

Flavor: Toasted hazelnuts, honey taste, caramel finish, delicate, almost no tannin

Anji White Needle
Anji Bai Cha

From: Zhejiang Province, Anji County, China

Appearance: Long, slender, needle-shaped leaves that are pale-green almost white in color

Harvested: The leaf is whitish-green in color when plucked in early spring, mid-April to mid-May.

Processed: The shoots are hand-worked to form flat, thick blades, then the tea is basket-fired.

Details: In Chinese, "Bai" means white. This tea is called Anji Bai (white tea) despite the fact that this is a green tea. When infused, the tea unfurls into a single pale green leaf set with one bud and one leaf. This pricey tea is rich in amino acids.

Steeping: 170-180°F, 1 to 2 minutes

Liquor: Clear, pale green, pale yellow, crystal clear

Aroma: Fresh, slightly vegetal, grass, asparagus

Flavor: Smooth, sweet, woodsy, earthy, long vegetal finish; delicate, hint of orchid, pine nut or fruit, slightly acidic

Yellow Mountain Hair Tip
Huang Shan Mao Feng

From: The slopes of Yellow Mountain (Huang Shan) in Anhui Province, China

Appearance: The slightly twisted, tender, young shoots are pointed and covered with delicate white down.

Harvested: Mid-April, hand-plucked, 1 bud and 1 to 2 leaves

Processed: Sometimes pan-fired, sometimes dried in an oven

Details: This tea, one of China's Ten Most Famous Teas, was first harvested in Huang Shan in the middle of the Ming Dynasty (1368–1644).

Steeping: 175°F, 3 minutes – can infuse multiple times

Liquor: Light, brilliant clear gold

Aroma: Sorrel, raw vegetables, "intense"

Flavor: Delicate, silky, notes of green beans and artichoke, flowery, sweet lingering aftertaste

Precious Eyebrows
Chun Mei, Chun Mee, Zhen Mei or Mei Cha

From: This tea is made in every tea-producing province in China.

Appearance: Long, fine, jade green leaves

Harvested: Bud and one leaf or bud and two leaves, in spring

Processed: Hand-rolled in the shape of eyebrows

Details: Outside China it's often called Young Hyson or Hyson. This was probably the first loose leaf tea and is still the commonest green tea.

Steeping: 160°F, 3 minutes

Liquor: Pale yellow or egg-yolk color

Aroma: Woody accents

Flavor: Smooth taste, plum-like

Fur Tip
Xin Yang Mao Xian

From: High mountain area in Xin Yang county of Henan Province, China

Appearance: Dark green, pointed leaves

Harvested: Picked in early spring

Processed: The leaves of this green tea are rolled by hand.

Details: One of the Ten Most Famous Teas of China, this tea is seldom available outside China.

Steeping: 160°F, 3 minutes

Liquor: Orangey-green or emerald color
Aroma: Fresh, heady
Flavor: Smooth

Sunflower Seed or Melon Seed
Lu An Gua Pian

From: Anhui Province, China
Appearance: Long, twisted leaves with bluish hues
Harvested: Difficult to manufacture, the leaves are plucked carefully, including the single first leaf below the bud.
Processed: Basket-fired
Details: Lu An Gua Pian was offered as a Tribute Tea to the Ming Dynasty Imperial Court.
Steeping: 160-175°F, 2 to 3 minutes
Liquor: Deep straw, golden yellow
Aroma: Mineral, biscuit aftertaste
Flavor: Intense, sweet taste, earthy, clean, soft; flowery, fruity notes. Known for its concentration of flavor

Curled Dragon Silver Tips
Pan Long Yin Hao

From: Zhejiang Province, China
Appearance: Spiral leaf with a large, fuzzy, white tip
Harvested: End of March, early April
Processed: Pan-fired
Details: One of the smoothest green teas, the tightly crimped spirals unfurl during steeping. This tea is produced in limited quantities.
Steeping: 170-180°F, 2 to 3 minutes
Liquor: Pale straw color, pale yellow-green
Aroma: Clean, earthy, meadow-like
Flavor: Vegetal, lightly-sweetened cocoa, honeyed finish

Brown Rice Tea or Popcorn Tea
Genmaicha

From: Shizuoka prefecture in Japan
Appearance: Needle-like Sencha or Bancha leaves are mixed with toasted brown rice for this medium-quality tea with low tannin content.
Harvested: Harvested like Bancha leaves, after the second flush
Processed: Oven-fired
Details: Genmaicha, the most popular Japanese green tea abroad, mixes well with East Asian foods. Sometimes matcha is added, covering the leaf and rice with green powder, and the tea is called "matcha genmaicha."
Steeping: 170-190°F, 2 to 3 minutes
Liquor: Clear green, with olive hue or light brown
Aroma: Spicy, warm, smell of toasted rice
Flavor: Toasty, nutty; deep vegetal flavor of Sencha with toastiness of roasted brown rice, hazelnut taste

Twig Tea or Stalk Tea
Kukicha

From: Shizuoka prefecture in Japan
Appearance: Consists of stems and stalks normally discarded in the production of Sencha, Gyokuro and Matcha teas
Processed: Young stems and stalks of the tea plant are steamed, then stems are separated and dried.
Harvested: Made in early spring
Details: The twig tea produced from the stalks of Gyokuro is known as "Karigane" or Karigane Sencha and is highly prized.
Steeping: 175°F, 2 to 3 minutes
Liquor: Brilliant green, with hints of yellow
Aroma: Light fragrance, fresh, herbaceous aroma
Flavor: Smooth, velvety, clean taste, refreshing

Matcha

From: Produced in Aichi prefecture, Japan, since the 1200s (also produced in Kagoshima, Kyoto and Shizuoka)

Appearance: Powdered green tea

Harvested: When new shoots on the tea bush have two or three leaves, they are shaded from sunlight for two–three weeks, producing more chlorophyll in the leaves.

Processed: The leaves are dried after steaming, but not rolled. During drying, all leaf veins and fine stems are removed from the leaves and ground into a fine powder.

Details: Matcha, the only tea produced from powdered leaves, was introduced by Buddhist monks around 1000 CE. The powder completely dissolves when whisked into water with a bamboo whisk or chasen, producing a frothy liquor. The leaf is grown under 90% shade and has more antioxidants than other green teas.

Ceremonial grade or premium grade matcha is used in the Japanese tea ceremony, Chanoyu. Culinary grade or lower grade matcha is used in cooking. Lighter green varieties are sweeter, the darker ones more astringent. The leaf is consumed in its entirety, providing more nutrients. Matcha is the most perishable form of tea and is generally sold in small, sealed, tin containers. The best matcha is very expensive with small tins selling for $40–$80. Culinary grade matcha is a good value and is used for confections, ice cream, baking and for a modestly-priced cup of tea. Koicha (thick tea) = 2 tsp. matcha, 2 oz. water, gives a deep flavor. Usucha (thin tea) = 1 tsp. matcha, 3 oz. water, tastes light and astringent.

Steeping: Use 1 tsp. of matcha per 8 oz. water. Pour a small amount of 175°F water over matcha and make a paste, then add the rest of the water and whisk briskly with a bamboo whisk (chasen) for 30 seconds until a dense foam appears.

Liquor: Bright, dark jade or emerald green with intensely green and cloudy "jade froth"

Aroma: Scent of herbs and new-mown hay, honeydew melon

Flavor: Astringent, sour taste of leaves, lingering, slightly bitter aftertaste, vegetal, intense spinach, artichoke

Precious Dew, Jade Dew or Pearl Dew

Gyokuro

From: Shizuoka prefecture, Japan

Appearance: Emerald-colored leaves are flat and pointed with a twisted needle.

Harvested: Plucked by hand and harvested once a year from the middle of May to mid-June

Processed: After plucking, the leaf is rapidly steamed and processed into flat-pointed needles of dark green.

Details: Three weeks before harvest, the tea plants are covered with sheets or nets to shade the plants. This increases chlorophyll production by reducing natural photosynthesis in the leaves, coaxing added sweetness from the leaf. This connoisseur's Japanese green tea is revered in Japan for purity of flavor. Developed and first sold in Japan in 1835 by the Yamamoto tea dynasty, the most famous Gyokuro-growing region is Uji, followed by Okabe in Shizuoka prefecture and the Yame district in Fukuoka prefecture, which is the country's largest producer of Gyokuro. Gyokuro is the highest grade of tea produced in Japan, and at just under 1% of the country's total tea production, it's one of the world's costliest teas.

Steeping: 160-165°F, 1 to 3 minutes

Liquor: Pale emerald, green-yellow, dark green

Aroma: Subtle perfume, fresh, green, like kelp or spinach

Flavor: Smooth taste, soft, not astringent, vegetal and robust, umami (savory) flavor, intense, complex

OOLONG TEAS

Phoenix Mountain, Phoenix Oolong or Phoenix Single Tree
Feng Huang Dan Cong

From: Fenghuang Shan (Phoenix Mountain) in the Wu Dong region of Guangdong Province, China

Appearance: Long, dark golden strips of leaf with reddish brown edges and a slight twist

Harvested: Leaves come from tall, ancient tea trees that grow wild; some trees are said to be close to 200 years old. Feng Huang Dan Cong is gathered with tall ladders, and the tea is plucked once a year in spring

Processed: A long wither followed by a heavy roasting

Details: There are several varieties, with individual "fragrances," such as cinnamon, almond and orchid. This tea is 70-80% oxidized and is brewed by the Chinese in tiny pots. Local cultivars are tall, single-trunk trees with branches that open like an umbrella. This tea is thought to be a Song Dynasty Tribute tea.

Steeping: 195-200°F, 1 to 3 minutes – can do multiple infusions

Liquor: Pale orangey-brown, golden yellow, amber orange

Aroma: Full, rich fragrance, strong, peachy, sweet and intense, floral notes

Flavor: Deep, fruity-ripe, apricots or spiced peaches; dense, velvety, intense flowery notes

Goddess of Mercy or Iron Goddess of Mercy
Ti Kuan Yin, Tiguanyin or Tieguanyin

From: Ti Kuan Yin is grown in northern part of Taiwan and in Anxi County in Fujian Province, China.

Appearance: Fleshy, oval leaves

Harvested: Two to three leaves are plucked by hand.

Processed: The brilliant green leaves are tightly rolled to form pearls. The hand-rolling shapes the leaf and pressing releases the plant's juice. This tea is partially oxidized, anywhere from 35-70%, depending on the desired flavor profile.

Details: With a history of over 200 years, this oolong tea is called "monkey picked," because the wild-grown tea is grown in hard to reach locations. It's one of China's Ten Most Famous Teas or Tribute Teas. Taiwanese Ti Kuan Yin teas are large, somewhat loose semi-balled shaped teas, Ti Kuan Yin is used in the Gong Fu tea ceremony.

Steeping: 185-195°F, 2 to 4 minutes. Can steep repeatedly as infusions will vary from light to clear and rich. Leaves will swell and open gradually. Pour on hot water, immediately pour off and let the leaves breathe, then pour on water again and steep for 2 to 3 minutes.

Liquor: Golden amber to brownish green; golden, soft, velvety

Aroma: Very fresh, fruit fragrance (apricots or peaches), flowery notes of jasmine, orchid, lily of the valley

Flavor: Low tannin, not astringent, fruity, deep, richly sweet, creamy sweetness

Rock Tea
Wu Yi Shan or Wuyi Shan

From: Grows wild in a range of mountain peaks in the northern Fujian Province on China's south coast. The area is a UNESCO World Heritage site.

Appearance: Strip-style oolong

Harvested: Three to four separate leaves are plucked once a year in the spring, mid-April to mid-May.

Processed: Traditional Wu Yi Shan rock oolong teas are still made entirely by hand.

Details: The tea plants grow amid the rocky terrain, providing the plants with vital minerals and nutrients. The Wu Yi range acts as a natural barrier against cold northern winds while retaining the warm, moist air from the south. This is one of the most expensive teas due to limited production.

Steeping: 190°F, 3 to 4 minutes – can do multiple infusions
Liquor: Orange-yellow, dark amber
Aroma: Sweet, floral
Flavor: Hints of smokiness, stone fruit flavor

Water Sprite
Shui Xian or Hsien

From: This large-leaf oolong comes from a tall, single-trunk tree.
Appearance: The leaves are a thick, glossy, dark, shiny green with buds that are fat, yellow-green and covered in hairs.
Harvested: Top 3 to 4 leaves are picked in the morning after sunrise.
Processed: The Shui Xian leaf can also be processed into black or white tea.
Details: One of China's famous Tribute Teas. The loose, twisted or rolled strips of leaf are used in the Gong Fu tea ceremony.
Steeping: 190-205°F, 5 to 7 minutes
Liquor: Clear, orangey-brown or bronze liquor
Aroma: Orchid
Flavor: Slightly spicy flavor; strong, full-bodied; fresh, fruity aftertaste; woody, fruity orchid notes in aftertaste

White Tip or Oriental Beauty
Bai Hao

From: Originally called Formosa Oolong, this oolong is grown near Taipei in Nantou or in Hsinchu prefecture in Taiwan at lower elevations from 650 to 1600 feet.
Appearance: The fine, dark red, twisted leaves are dotted with silver buds.
Harvested: Harvested once a year during the first 15 days of July
Processed: A tiny insect, the leaf hopper, bites the tea leaf, which then begins an enzymatic process, improving the quality of the tea. Only the bitten leaves are plucked and, when processed, the leaves turn red-brown with white tips.

Details: This is Taiwan's premier oolong and most famous tea with quite limited production. The white-haired buds undergo 35-40% oxidation. The most prized of all classic fancy Formosa oolongs, this tea is usually served in small porcelain cups with a light-colored inside. A version developed in Taiwan after World War II is sometimes marketed to the West as Champagne Oolong.

Steeping: 180-195°F, 3 to 4 minutes

Liquor: Coppery, clear liquor, pale golden color, brilliant amber

Aroma: Aromatic complexity; honeyed, floral, stone fruit notes (apricots and peaches) or notes of orchid and muscat grape, apple, nutmeg, honey

Flavor: Velvety, sweet, fresh "honeyed fruit" – peaches, honey, spices, wild orchid, floral

Formosa Oolong
(see also Bai Hao Oolong)

From: Grown at elevations well below 500 feet at northern end of Taiwan near Taipei

Appearance: Twisted leaves in various earth tones

Harvested: The beautiful white-tipped leaves of this tea are picked during late spring.

Processed: Traditionally 50-60% oxidation

Details: Formosa Oolong is the traditional trade name for Taiwan's classic tea. This tea is usually very expensive. Formosa Great Oolong, Pouchong, is a lighter form of oolong which can be infused several times.

Steeping: 200-212°F, 3 to 4 minutes

Liquor: Light copper or clear golden

Aroma: Clean, "exquisite" aroma, nutty, apricots or buttered toast

Flavor: Delicate, toasted walnuts, sweet vegetal notes

Frozen Peak or Icy Peak
Tung Ting or Dong Ding

From: Grown in Nantou County, Taiwan, dating back to 1855 and named after the Tung Ting or Dong Ding Mountains

Appearance: The dark green leaves are tightly folded or rolled into balls.

Harvested: The harvest seasons are April-June and September-November.

Processed: 10-15% oxidized

Details: This is one of the most famous and finest of Formosa oolongs, and there are almost 4000 growers of this tea. The slow-growing winter and spring teas are considered best. Tung Ting is traditionally steeped Gong Fu style in a gaiwan. Often referred to as Orchid or Jade Oolong, this is one of the most highly regarded oolongs, and it commands a premium price because of high worldwide demand.

Steeping: 180-200°F, 5 to 7 minutes or 205-212°F, 3 to 4 minutes

Liquor: Orangey-green, golden-green yellow, dark yellow, light gold

Aroma: Complex, clean, fresh, caramel, chestnut aroma, lilac, clover, honey; leather and tobacco notes, intense flowery-vanilla. Low tannin

Flavor: Smooth, light taste, nutty and sweet; floral aftertaste, ripe peach, buttery, lush mouthful, creamy, underlying vegetal

Baozhong or Pouchong

From: Grown in the Pinglin, Shinlin, Wenshan or Hsientien Townships in Taipei County, Taiwan

Appearance: Long, open-twist leaf

Harvested: Leaves are picked in both spring and winter.

Processed: Oven-fired and roasted with minimal processing, 12-18% oxidized

Details: A way of packaging that originated in 1860, Baozhong refers to oolong tea packaged in elongated papers or "paper wrapped." The Taiwan Pinglin Tea Industry Museum offers tea education.

Steeping: 180-195°F, 3-4 minutes – can do multiple infusions

Liquor: Delicate, pale golden yellow color to amber; soft, sweet, fresh, greenish-yellow

Aroma: "Pure tea" fragrance, fresh, subtle, highly floral

Flavor: Smooth, creamy, rich, buttery, no astringency, low tannin. Sweet aftertaste, flowery

Green Heart
Qing Xin, Cingshin or Luan Ze

From: A popular oolong varietal from Nantou, Taiwan, this tea is planted at high altitude in rich soil.

Appearance: The small, dense tea bush has leaves with pronounced veins.

Harvested: Various harvest times depending on altitude

Processed: Withered and tightly rolled

Details: Qing Xin was used in 40% of Taiwan's tea plantations. There is not a high yield, so this tea is more expensive.

Steeping: 190-195°F, 1 minute – for multiple infusions, add a minute to the steeping time with each infusion.

Liquor: Clear, pale yellow

Aroma: "Green, crisp pastoral notes" with hints of mountain flowers

Flavor: Floral, vegetal sweet tropical flavor – intensely sweet. Mouthfeel is smooth, not too thick, not at all dry. First note is mellow, slightly toasted, yeasty, bready; later note has a honey sweetness with a creamy texture and taste.

BLACK TEAS

Golden Monkey
Panyang Gong Fu or Panyang Congou

From: Fujian Province in China

Appearance: Long, black, twisted leaf with significant tip

Harvested: The bud and the first leaf are picked in spring and fall.

Processed: Rolled by hand or gently rolled by machine

Details: This classic south China congou was first produced in 1851 and was very successful in Europe. Little known in America, Panyang Gong Fu is sold primarily to England, the Middle East and Russia.

Steeping: 190-212°F, 3 to 5 minutes

Liquor: Dark amber, copper-colored, raw sienna

Aroma: Slight earthiness, nutty

Flavor: Smooth, deep, slightly malty, complex, layered, soft, no astringency

Keemun
Qimen

From: Qimen in Anhui Province, China

Appearance: A "gongfu" or congou, this high-quality tea has tight, small, black leaves.

Harvested: Eight to ten days in late April and early May

Processed: Seared over hot woks or in ovens

Details: This fragrant black tea is one of China's Ten Most Famous Teas. The tea is grown in a temperate climate with abundant rainfall. Keemun is sometimes referred to as the "Queen of all teas" because some sources say this is a favorite at Buckingham Palace. For years, Keemun was considered the best Chinese black tea and called the "King of Red Tea" or "Burgundy" of China tea. Available in various grades and shapes, the best ones are called Keemun Mao Feng, Keemun Hao Ya and Keemun Congou.

Steeping: 185-205°F, 5 to 7 minutes or 205-212°F, 3 to 4 minutes
Liquor: Brilliant red or rich brown liquor, classic copper color, thick, full liquor
Aroma: Delicate scent of orchids; delicate earthy, like chocolate; complex bouquet of flowers, cocoa, leather
Flavor: Brisk, "winey," sweet flavor, like orchid; deep, rich, aromatic, cocoa-like, chocolaty, soft, velvety, no astringency

Black Dragon or Red Plum
Jiuqu Wuling, Jiuqu Wulong or Jiu Hongmei

From: Mt. Dawu in Zhejiang Province, China
Appearance: Fine, tight twists or hook-like rolls of leaf
Harvested: In the spring, mid- to late April
Processed: Second flush, around mid- to late April
Details: The name Jiuqu means Nine-Bend Stream or Nine-Bend Red Plum. This gongfu black tea gives a coppery red liquor. Black Dragon is sometimes called an oolong.
Steeping: 203°F, 5 to 7 minutes
Liquor: Coppery-red
Aroma: Honey sweet, mild floral, berries or plums
Flavor: Mellow, subtle, refreshing taste, smooth floral aftertaste

Lapsang Souchong
(Souchong means "Small Leaf Varietal")

From: Fujian Province, China and also in Taiwan
Appearance: Crepey, large open twist leaf
Harvested: Fourth or fifth leaves of the tea plant are plucked.
Processed: Fully oxidized, smoked over pine or resinous wood or scented with pinewood smoke
Details: According to records, Lapsang Souchong is the first black tea ever produced. The one and only original comes from high up in the Wuyi Mountains in Tong Mu Guan, where it is still made by the Jiang family. Lapsang Souchong is often referred to as Tarry Lapsang and is made primarily for export. The Taiwanese style is stronger and more heavily

smoked, while the Fujian version is milder and softer. Some people like to blend a small amount of Lapsang Souchong into other leaf teas to add just a bit of smoke.

Steeping: 190-210°F, 2 to 5 minutes

Liquor: Amber to burnt sienna, coppery, rich, red

Aroma: Sweet smokiness, covers the other aromas in the leaves

Flavor: Biscuity, lightly to robustly smoked flavor, pinewood, low level of tannin

Yunnan

Dianhong or "South of the Clouds"

From: Yunnan (Dian) Province in China

Appearance: Fat buds and shoots with thick soft leaves

Harvested: Sometimes made exclusively from golden shoots or buds, the quality is determined by the amount of golden buds and the amount of broken leaf.

Processed: This tea is also known as hongcha or "red tea" because oxidation turns the leaves a red color.

Details: Yunnan is thought to be the original home of the Camellia Sinensis species, and some 260 of the world's 380 tea varietals are found in Yunnan. Yunnan Buds of Gold and Yunnan Golden Needles are among the highest grades of Yunnan black tea, with long tips and a malty, sweet liquor.

Steeping: 195-205°F, 4 to 7 minutes

Liquor: Deep golden, amber-red, dark caramel

Aroma: Fruity, flowery, honeyed notes, nutty, earthiness

Flavor: Earthy, maple sweetness, smooth, full-bodied

Ceylon

From: Sri Lanka

Appearance: Long, curly leaves are nearly black

Harvested: Plucked from late June to the end of August in the eastern districts and from the beginning of February to mid-March in western districts

Processed: Withered, rolled, oxidized, fired and dried

Details: Ceylon is the colonial name of the island of Sri Lanka. The tea industry is the largest employer in Sri Lanka. There are approximately 650 tea estates covering almost 482,000 acres. Well-known tea regions in Sri Lanka include Galle, Kandy, Nuwara Eliya, Datnapura, Dimbula, Uva, Ruhana and Uda Pussellawa. The Uva region is known for high-grown (4000 feet) or "grand crus" tea. Nuwara Eliya high-grown teas are sometimes referred to as the "Darjeelings of Ceylon." Ceylons are labeled by region, district, estate and grade, and Ceylon teas are often used in tea blends. Ceylon Golden Buds is one of the world's priciest teas and is produced in minute quantities.

Steeping: 185-205°F, 3 to 5 minutes

Liquor: Golden orange coppery, pale yellow to dark brown

Aroma: Woody, fruity; mildly peppery, light, delicate

Flavor: Brisk, sweet, slightly astringent; citrus spice; hints of oranges and cloves

Darjeeling
The Champagne of Teas – India's Most Celebrated Tea

From: West of the Assam area in the northern state of West Bengal in Darjeeling, in the foothills of the Himalayas of northeast India

Appearance: Smaller leaves, because the cool, thin air slows leaf growth concentrating the flavor in the leaf.

Harvested: Hand-picked

Processed: Fully oxidized

Details: Tea plantations were first recorded in Darjeeling in 1856. By 1866, there were 39 tea gardens in Darjeeling. By 1881, there were over 100. Due to garden closings by the early 2000s, the number of tea estates in Darjeeling has dwindled to 75. Long, cold winters and cool, breezy summers provide ideal climate for this high-mountain tea, and this complex tea demands higher prices. The Tea Board of India introduced distinctive logos for three main specialty teas—Darjeeling, Assam and Nilgiri—to ensure 100% pure tea. The Darjeeling Planters Association was formed in 1983, and only teas from gardens within a certain area of the Darjeeling region are allowed to legally carry the green circular Darjeeling logo, which signifies 100% Darjeeling tea. Some famous estates include: Castleton Estate, Gopaldhara, Jungpana, Margaret's Hope, Seeyok (organic first flush), Goomtee, Makaibari, Mullootor, Puttabong and Ambootia. The annual output of Darjeeling tea is 1% of India's total tea production.

First Flush: early spring; mid-March to second week of May – light-bodied teas, with a sweet aftertaste. First flush Darjeelings are often treated like Beaujolais Nouveau wines, i.e., eagerly awaited harvest sometimes sent by air.

In-between Flush: April and May – these teas are not widely available.

Second Flush: Late spring–early summer; end of June until mid-July; firmer leaves, longer oxidation, full-bodied liquor, malty fragrance

Summer/Monsoon Flush: Coarse leaf for commercial tea blends, astringent, more mature flavor

Autumn Flush: October and November. Winter is dormant period.

Steeping: 190-212°F, 3 to 5 minutes

Liquor: Pale to medium golden yellow to bright copper (dark orange) color, yellow brown

Aroma: Crisp, fresh notes; sharply fresh and floral, hints of ginger and citrus notes

Flavor: First flush Darjeelings have a flavor called "muscatel"; fruity notes of grapes, plums, pineapple, grapefruit or apricots. Darjeelings generally do not go well with citrus.

Assam
Camellia sinensis assamica

From: Grown on both sides of the Brahamaputra Valley in India, the birthplace of India's indigenous tea bush
Appearance: Regular, large leaves and golden shoots
Harvested: Large, whole-leaf, single-leaf pluck
Processed: Fully-oxidized
Details: The native tea tree was discovered by the British in this northeast corner of India, 120 miles east of Darjeeling, and is the single largest tea growing region in the world. Tea production in Assam is year round due to the tropical weather: tropical rains, high humidity and heat. Assam is 60-75% of India's total tea production, and the majority of Assam is produced into CTC and used for tea blends and in chai. The distinct Assam logo is an image of the one-horned rhino that lives in the Brahmaputra Valley. Assam, this classic black Indian tea with full-bodied taste, is the tea most often used for "British taste" teas, and it can take a splash of milk.
Steeping: 190-212°F, 3 to 5 minutes
Liquor: Burnt sienna color, coppery, clear, dark red liquor, dark amber, orange-red
Aroma: Nutty and herbaceous, spicy, malty
Flavor: Brisk, smooth, biscuit, robust, malty, full-bodied, ideal for blends, caramel-buttery, notes of papaya and mango

Nilgiri
Blue Mountains

From: Tamil Nadu and Kerala in South India's Blue Hills or Blue Mountains
Appearance: Twisted leaves of a dark chestnut brown
Harvested: The prime plucking season or Winter Flush is December-March, and the tea is called "frost tea" because of the threat of frost in the valleys.

Processed: Most Nilgiri production is made into CTC and is consumed locally.

Details: The tea industry was established here in 1840. The tea geographic area is 35 miles long and 20 miles wide, with more than 148,000 acres of tea and comprising 10% of India's total tea production. The tea is grown on high ridges, some reaching 8200 feet. Two monsoons a year give the bushes wet and dry seasons. A light, daily coating of frost slows plant growth and concentrates flavor. Tea is plucked all year long, but spring- and winter-plucked make up 65% of the tea production here. Pure Nilgiri is assured by the logo which depicts the hills of the Blue Mountains of Southern India.

Nilgiri Coonoor Tea is part of a growing trend toward specialty teas with organic cultivation. One of the first tea estates, Thiashola, was established in 1859 and, still in production today, it acquired organic certification in 2003. There are more than 20,000 small landowners in six districts: Panthalur, Gudalur, Kothagiri, Coonor, Kundah and Udhagamandalam. 50% of Nilgiri tea is exported to the U.K., Europe and the Commonwealth of Independent States. The Nilgiri Planters Association, established in 1891, works with the large tea gardens to help maintain the high quality of their teas.

Steeping: 195-212°F, 3 to 5 minutes

Liquor: Clear copper to pale amber

Aroma: Light, fresh

Flavor: Crisp, mineral, mellow taste. Bright, brisk, smooth, rounded mellow flavor

PU-ERH TEAS

Sheng
(pronounced like "young," means raw or uncooked)

From: Yunnan Province in China

Appearance: Open leaf and buds compressed into cakes

Harvested: Large leaves are pan-fired, rolled and then dried in the sun.

Processed: Pu-erh tea undergoes a natural post-production fermentation. Living organisms on the surface of the tea leaves combined with humidity and time results in mellowing of the astringent leaf. Open leaf and buds are compressed into individually wrapped cakes, marked with information detailing the village or tea factory that manufactured it. Pu-erh is sometimes sold as loose leaf tea.

Details: Produced in a lush, subtropical and mountainous region where many of the tea plants qualify as being ancient because they're more than a hundred years old. Pu-erh is slowly aged or fermented over a long period of time. It can be drunk young, but it acquires the best flavor after a decade of aging. Sheng teas are considered fully mature after aging for 30 years. This tea is often used for digestive properties and cleansing action, and is known as a slimming tea. Break off chunks from the tea cake for steeping. It's said that pu-erh tastes "of the earth."

Steeping: 195-203°F, 3 to 5 minutes; Before steeping, rinse the tea in hot water for five seconds to start opening the leaves. Then pour the water off and add fresh hot water for steeping.

Liquor: Dark, burnt umber, golden amber hue

Aroma: Lightly herbaceous, clean fragrance of forest

Flavor: Robust, smooth, sweet, deep woodsy flavor, likened to "forest-floor," tastes of the earth, "beef broth," mushrooms, tobacco

Shou

(pronounced like "show," means ripe or cooked)

From: Yunnan Province in China

Appearance: Commonly found in loose leaf form or compressed cakes

Harvested: Large leaves are pan-fired, rolled and then dried in the sun.

Processed: Because of the demand for pu-erh, in the 1970s a new type of tea, "Shou" or "cooked," was developed. It's made in tea factories using the "wo dui" process of artificially accelerated fermentation. The leaves are spread in a deep pile, dampened with mists of water, and a thermal blanket is placed over the leaves to encourage a rapid fermentation of 45–70 days. Heat encourages natural bacteria and stimulates fermentation.

Details: Shou pu-erh is meant for immediate consumption, and the flavor improves only slightly with aging. This tea is considered a dietary supplement to help stimulate digestion, help with weight loss and help eliminate bad cholesterol. Shou pu-erh is more reasonably priced than sheng pu-erh.

Steeping: Rinse with hot water twice for 5 seconds each time then infuse at 205-210°F for 30 seconds; add 5 seconds for each infusion up to 10 infusions

Liquor: Burnt umber, with red-orange hue

Aroma: Bold, earth, like damp leaves, mushrooms or forest floor or tree bark

Flavor: Earthy taste, smooth, deep, more "fermented" taste

Glossary of Tea Terms

A

Agony of the leaves: "the writhing, swirling action of the loose tea leaves immersed in boiling water" (quote from Helen Gustafson). For the best view, use a clear glass teapot.

Antioxidant: abundant in the tea plant, these compounds help to neutralize cell-damaging free radicals

Aroma: the tea's scent, either of the infused leaf or the steeped result. Aroma is usually described with analogies to fruit, flowers or nuts.

Assam: a major tea production region in northeastern India, one of the largest tea growing regions in the world; the name of the full-bodied, malty tea from this region

Astringency: the quality of the tea's liquor that gives a bite or piquancy to the taste; dry, puckery sensation in the mouth noticeable in more oxidized teas

Autumnal flush: tea affected by cold weather and produced in the fall; leaves picked late in the harvest which is October–November

B

Bai Mudan: white peony tea; originated in Fujian Province, China; a popular style of white tea containing a bud and first two leaves

Baicha: see white tea

Baked or Bakey: unpleasant taste caused by firing tea leaves at a temperature that is too high; a negative, dry, overcooked taste

Basket-fired: an artisanal Japanese tea process traditionally used in the manufacture of green and yellow teas. To prevent oxidation, fresh leaf is fired or dried in a basket.

Bergamot: a Mediterranean citrus fruit; a fragrant oil extracted from the rind of the fruit which is the source of orange essence used to flavor Earl Grey tea

Bi Luo Chun or Green Snail Spring: a tightly spiraled green tea first made in Jiangsu Province, China; one of China's Ten Most Famous teas

Bingcha or Beeng Cha: cake tea or tea cake, a disk-shaped, compressed form of pu-erh tea; traditionally, a unit of measure for pu-erh, approximately 357 grams

Biscuity: an aromatic term used for well-fired Assam teas, indicating the presence of the signature malty taste that Assam teas should possess

Bitter: an unpleasant biting taste that usually results from over-steeping tea

Black tea: the type of tea made from fully-oxidized leaves; the most widely-consumed tea in India, Sri Lanka and the West

Blend: combination of various types of tea from diverse locations to achieve a consistent, desired flavor profile

Body: the viscosity or mouthfeel in the tea liquor, can be full, light, moderate; the overall depth of flavor

Bohea: former term used by European merchants for early Chinese oolong and black teas, a mispronunciation of Wuyi

Bouquet: the ensemble of smells perceived by the nose, usually referring to fragrant teas

Brassy: refers to tea liquor with a bitter, metallic taste

Brick tea: pu-erh tea leaves which have been steamed and highly compressed into a brick shape

Bright: indicates a clean, clear style that refreshes the palate; sparkling characteristic of the liquors of all fine teas

Brisk: a tasting term to describe a lively, slightly astringent sensation; a pleasant trait associated with all fine black teas

Burnt: undesirable taste of leaves that have been overfired during processing

C

Caffeine: a bitter alkaloid produced by the tea plant which deters insect attacks; a naturally occurring chemical which acts as a stimulant and diuretic in humans

Camellia sinensis: an evergreen shrub whose leaves and leaf buds are used to produce tea. The two major varieties grown today are C. sinensis, var. sinensis and C. sinensis, var. assamica.

Catechin: a type of polyphenol and powerful antioxidant found in tea. A well-known example is epigallocatechin gallate, or EGCG.

Ceylon: colonial name for the island of Sri Lanka; also black tea with a brisk, bright flavor produced in Sri Lanka

Cha: Romanized spelling of Chinese and Japanese character which denotes the word "tea"

Chado: Japanese for the "way of tea," originally pronounced "sado"

Chai: word for tea in India; in the West, generally refers to masala chai, a sweetened black tea infused with milk and spices

Chanoyu: "hot water for tea"; the elaborate, formal Japanese tea ceremony which dictates certain movements and equipment for the making and serving of matcha

Chasen: a small whisk constructed of a single piece of bamboo that has been sliced into fine tines. It is used to whisk matcha with water.

Chashaku: a small bamboo scoop used to measure matcha into a tea bowl

Chawan: Japanese for "tea bowl"; a bowl used to whisk matcha

Congou: former term for Chinese black tea; mispronunciation of gong fu

Creamy: refers to a tea that is round in the mouth and slightly oily

Crepey: crimped, crepe-like appearance characteristic of OP (orange pekoe) teas

CTC: Crush-Tear-Curl, also called Cut-Tear-Curl; a machine process invented in 1930 in which tea leaves are chopped into uniform particles to speed processing and facilitate oxidation; typical of most black tea grown in India and other lowland producing countries and used in bagged tea to create a rapidly infusing, more darkly colored tea. CTC production is prevalent in Africa, most of Assam, parts of South India and Indonesia.

Cultivar: combination of words "cultivated" and "variety"; a unique member of a species created by human intervention to fulfill a specific trait or particular characteristic; may be designed to be disease resistant, drought resistant, a particular color, taste or shape

D

Dan Cong: (pronounced dan song); familiar term used by tea enthusiasts to describe the grade of highly oxidized oolong tea produced from the Feng Huang Dan Cong single-trunk trees in Guangdong Province, China

Darjeeling: fragrant tea produced in the mountainous Darjeeling region of West Bengal, India; often called the "champagne of teas," represents 1% of the total tea production of India

Dust: smallest grade of black tea, typically low value/low quality; used for quick extraction and to give strength to teas in commercial-grade tea bags

E

Earl Grey: a strong black tea blend flavored with bergamot oil; named for England's Earl Grey, Charles Grey (1764-1845); the West's most popular scented tea

Earthy: term used to describe the earthy flavor of some teas, the result of the growing conditions in a particular tea-growing region or storage in damp conditions

Epigallocatechin gallate (EGCG): a catechin present in large concentrations in green tea; mentioned in many academic studies as a super-antioxidant and responsible for the positive health benefits of green tea

F

Fang cha: square-shaped, compressed brick of pu-erh tea

Fannings: small particles of tea, one grade larger than dust; commonly used in tea bags for a quick-steeping infusion

Fermentation: term used in tea manufacture to indicate oxidation; also refers to the maturation process of pu-erh tea

Firing: process in which tea leaves are heated and/or dried to prevent further enzymatic changes or oxidation; renders tea shelf-stable, fit for packing and storing

Flush: the new growth on the tea bush that occurs several times during the plucking/harvest season; a unique plucking season, usually one of four throughout the year. Each flush is usually known for its unique flavor.

Frost tea: tea from around the Nilgiri Hills (the Blue Mountains) in southern India. Tea is harvested during the coldest months of winter when the tea estates are covered with mist and fog, which make the best quality Nilgiri teas.

Full in the mouth: a tasting term that denotes smoothness; giving a sensation of fullness that has a pleasing mouth-filling effect

G

Gaiwan or Guywan: Chinese ceramic lidded cup and saucer used to steep tea in China; originated around the year 1350. With practice, a tea drinker sips or pours from a gaiwan with only one hand.

Genmaicha: Japanese green tea blended with popped or roasted rice

Gong fu: a style of brewing tea using a high proportion of leaf to water and a series of short infusions; drinking tea from very small cups

Grand cru: "great production" or "great growth"; tea of the finest quality

Green tea: first style of tea ever produced; typical style of tea production in China and Japan. The leaf is heated shortly after harvest to halt oxidation.

Gyokuro or "jade dew" or "pearl dew" tea: a rich-flavored Japanese green tea made from plants shaded before harvest; represents under 1% of Japan's tea production

H

Heicha: "dark tea," a distinct style from China in which the leaves are aged and usually fermented; refers to a popular subcategory of pu-erh tea

Hojicha: roasted, twig-style green tea from Japan; contains little caffeine and tannin so Hojicha is a popular drink before sleep

Huang cha: see yellow tea

Hyson or young hyson: leaf description in green tea manufacture for larger OP-sized (orange pekoe) leaf grades. Originally describing China teas, the term is no longer used in China where these teas are called Chun Mee; it is often used for Indian green teas.

I–J

Infusion: the liquor made by soaking tea leaves in hot water; describes both the act of infusing and the wet leaves recovered from the process

Jasmine tea: typically a green or oolong tea scented with jasmine flowers or buds

Jin cha: "tight tea," a mushroom-shaped form of compressed pu-erh

K

Kabuse: "covered"; a special type of Sencha that is shaded for seven to ten days prior to harvest to alter the tea's chemical composition and attain a mellower flavor

Keemun: a rich Chinese black tea from Anhui Province, named after the town of Qimen; referred to as the "king of red tea" or the "burgundy" of Chinese tea

Koicha: "thick tea"; one of the two classic matcha preparations served during Chanoyu, the Japanese tea ceremony; traditionally served communally, with participants sharing the tea from one tea bowl

Kyusu: "teapot"; traditionally a kyusu is a Japanese teapot with a side handle, used for brewing green tea. Fine, slightly porous clays are used in making it, and interiors are often left unglazed so as to retain a little of the tea's flavor.

L

Lao cha: "old tea"; refers to an aged tea plant or an aged tea leaf used for ripe pu-erh tea

Lapsang Souchong: Chinese black tea from Fujian Province, fully oxidized and traditionally smoked over local pine wood; considered the first black tea ever made

Liquor: brewed tea or the liquor obtained by infusing tea leaves

Long Jing: "dragonwell," a classic Chinese green tea with distinctive sword-shaped leaves; grown around Hangzhou in the West Lake region of Zhejiang

L-theanine: a unique amino acid found in tea which can reduce stress, cause a "relaxed alertness" and induce a sense of well being

M

Malty: an underlying flavor usually associated with Assam and Yunnan teas

Mao cha: "raw tea," the semi-finished, sun-withered tea leaf that is the base for sheng and shou pu-erh tea

Mao feng: refers to the traditional premium green tea pluck of two leaves and a bud. Mao means "hair" and feng means "peak."

Mao jian: "hairpoint," a curly exceptional spring tea, also called "downy tip" which is a grading term; traditional premium green tea pluck consisting of one leaf and a bud

Matcha: "powdered tea"; a shaded, stone-ground Japanese green tea. Premium matcha is made from tencha, a special grade of Japanese green tea in which the stem and veins have been removed from the leaf. This yields an incredibly smooth and rich tea that is used for Chanoyu, the Japanese tea ceremony.

Mouthfeel: a description of the physical sensation of drinking tea, e.g., soft, astringent, creamy or full-bodied

Muscatel: a tasting term derived from grapes of the Muscat family; a flavor most often associated with Darjeelings, especially second flush Darjeelings

N

Nilgiri: "Blue Mountain," a mountain range in south India. Tea from this region equals about 10% of India's total tea production.

Nose: tasting term for the smell of the dry tea leaf; the aroma of brewed tea leaves or liquor

O

Oolong: derived from "wu long," the Chinese term for black dragon; a semi-oxidized type of tea traditionally made in China and Taiwan; usually ball shaped or twisted; renowned for its complex tastes and aromas and ability to be steeped several times

Orange pekoe: manufacturing term for the largest grade of black tea; grading term that refers to larger, unbroken tea leaves. Orange does not mean orange color, but instead refers to Holland's "House of Orange," the royal family of the first European country to import and re-export tea.

Oriental beauty: also known as bai hao or "white tip"; a heavily oxidized, deeply fragrant oolong from Taiwan that is bitten by the jassid or leaf-hopper insect before harvest, resulting in a chemical reaction that enhances the flavor of the tea

Orthodox manufacture: traditional whole-leaf tea manufacture; more expensive and time-consuming than CTC manufacture

Oven-fired (baked or roasted): an efficient drying and finish-firing combination often used in tea manufacture in which hot air is circulated through the tea

Oxidation: the term used for the chemical change due to a material's absorption of oxygen or a reaction with oxygen; the process of enzymatic browning in which elements in the tea leaves react with air, creating a dark brown-red color and characteristic deeper aroma and flavor in the tea

P

Pan-firing: method of manufacturing green tea which refers to a method of heating the leaf and arresting enzymatic oxidation of tea

Pekoe (often pronounced "peek-o," the proper pronunciation is "peck-oh"): term to describe the size of black tea leaves, also the fine hairs on the new tea buds

Phoenix oolong: also known as "dan cong" (pronounced dan song), a partially oxidized, twisted-leaf style of oolong native to the Phoenix Mountains in Guangdong Province, China

Plucking: picking and harvesting tea leaves from the plant. The bud-only, bud-set or as many as five or six leaves may be removed in a plucking.

Polyphenols: chemical compounds, also referred to as flavonoids, which are present in tea and have antioxidant qualities. Tea has around eight times more polyphenols than fruits and vegetables.

Pu-erh (also spelled pu-er, puer, pu'erh): a dark tea produced in China's Yunnan Province from the large leaf variety camellia sinensis assamica. Pu-erh is made in two main styles, sheng which is pronounced like "young" and shou which is pronounced like "show." Pu-erh is prized for its ability to gain complexity and value with proper aging and to be infused many times. The microbial process in pu-erh often continues for decades.

R

Rolling: process by which withered tea leaves are shaped and enzymatic oxidation is encouraged by rupturing the cell walls

S

Self-drinking: a tea with enough good characteristics such as aroma, body, flavor and color, that it can be enjoyed without blending it with other teas

Sencha: Japanese green tea that is steamed to deactivate the leaf enzymes. The classic taste profile of a well-made sencha tea is umami, often described as the fifth taste (savory) with characteristics of seaweed or mushrooms.

Sheng (pronounced like "young"): green or raw form of pu-erh; the original style of pu-erh which ages slowly and gains complexity over decades

Shou (pronounced like "show"): brown or ripe form of pu-erh in which additional moisture is introduced to the leaves; tends not to change as much as sheng when aged; invented in the 1970s

Silky: describes a smooth, slightly oily liquor, evocative of silk

Smoky: tasting term denoting a desirable characteristic of some Chinese teas, especially lapsang souchong

Smooth: having a pleasant, rounded taste

Specialty tea: high-grade loose leaf tea usually from small tea estates; segment of the tea industry that produces premium teas

Stale: faded aroma and a dead taste caused by excessive age and subsequent loss of quality

T

Tannins: chemical compounds found in tea; responsible for its dry taste

Tarry: a desirable smoky flavor caused by smoking tea leaves with wood or charcoal; most commonly associated with lapsang souchong

Tea: the second most consumed beverage in the world after water; the infused beverage brewed from the processed leaves of the camellia sinensis plant

Tea liquor: the tea infusion; the drinkable liquid produced when processed tea leaves have been steeped in water for the appropriate amount of time

Tencha: the Japanese green tea from which premium matcha is ground

Ten Famous Teas: teas formerly held in reserve for the Chinese emperors. Today these teas represent the premium growths and productions in their style. The list of Ten Famous Teas varies from time to time.

Terroir: combined influence of soil, climate, altitude and latitude of a particular tea growing region. Tea styles are sometimes named after their terroir.

Tetsubin: Japanese cast iron kettle generally used as a teapot. Tetsubin teapots heat evenly and retain heat well.

Theaflavin: yellow compounds formed during tea oxidation. Theaflavins bring brightness and briskness to the tea liquor.

Thearubigin: red and brown compounds formed by condensation of theaflavins during oxidation. Thearubigins are responsible for black tea's reddish liquor, body and strength.

Theanine: chemical unique to the tea plant, notable for its calming, yet not sedative effects; an amino acid unique to the tea plant; the older name for caffeine

Ti Kuan Yin or Tieguanyin ("goddess of mercy"): ball-shaped oolong produced in the Anxi area of Fujian Province, China as well as in Taiwan. Historically it had more oxidation and strength, but current style is lightly oxidized with a floral fragrance and is often prepared gong-fu style.

Tip: small unopened leaf of the tea plant; very end of the delicate young bud

Tippy: denotes tea that contains the bud-set or white or golden tips. Abundance of tips is indicative of careful plucking and denotes high quality.

Tisane: infused beverage from plants other than camellia sinensis; an herbal infusion made from the leaves, roots, seeds, fruit, flowers or bark of plants

Toasty: tasting term describing the aroma of a fine Keemun and other highly-fired teas caused by prolonged baking

Tuocha: Chinese for "bowl tea," a common shape for compressed pu-erh teas

Tribute tea: special teas, including the Ten Famous Teas, typically given as "tribute" to Chinese emperors; teas that in modern times have been found to be in high regard among Chinese tea scholars and experts

U

Umami: the word for the hard-to-describe fifth sense of taste that is often associated with mushrooms, soy sauce, broths or seaweed; a Japanese term for the savory flavor which is found in many steamed Japanese green teas

Usucha ("thin tea"): one of the two classic matcha preparations; served during Chanoyu, the Japanese tea ceremony, usually in individual bowls

W

White tea: the least processed type of tea, native to Fujian Province, China, in which the leaves are processed in only two steps, withering and drying

Winey: tasting term for complex flavor of black teas, particularly Keemun and Darjeeling

Withering: natural process of moisture evaporating from recently plucked tea leaves, making them suppler for further processing; generally done by spreading the leaves out, allowing air to pass over and through them

Wo Dui: "moisten pile," the process of adding additional moisture to pu-erh leaves in order to speed up fermentation; first attributed to the Kunming Tea Factory in Yunnan, China, in 1973

Yabukita: most common camellia sinensis cultivar used for over 85% of Japan's green tea production

Yancha: "cliff tea" or "rock tea"; a heavily-roasted style of twisted-leaf oolong produced in the Wuyi Mountains of Fujian Province, China; considered the first oolong ever made

Yellow tea or Huang Cha: type of tea similar to green tea in which oxidation is not completely halted. Tea leaves are piled, then covered or wrapped and kept damp until they turn yellow, then finished over low charcoal heat. Historically produced in Anhui Province, China

Yixing: region of China noted for its dark, purple clay for creating distinctive, small unglazed teapots often used for gong fu tea steeping style. A single type of tea is used for each pot, as the unglazed clay absorbs the taste of the tea over time.

Acknowledgement

With special gratitude to Linda Spangle—for introducing me to the Tea Time ladies, for sharing her writing expertise and always asking me the hard questions and, most of all, for her caring and support and friendship.

About the Author

Judith A. Leavitt, President
TalkingTea LLC

After earning a Master's Degree in Library Science, Judith Leavitt spent more than 30 years working in competitive intelligence, strategic planning and enterprise risk management in a major aerospace corporation. She achieved numerous awards for her work in advancing the field of competitive intelligence including membership in the prestigious CI Fellows. She is the author of three books on the topic of women in management.

Now the author has turned her energies to her lifelong passion for tea. A long-time member of the Specialty Tea Institute, she has completed work toward becoming a Certified Tea Specialist and has been named an Apprentice Tea Sommelier by renowned tea expert, James Norwood Pratt. She has collected and studied more than 300 books on tea and formed TalkingTea LLC to share her passion for tea and the tea lifestyle.

Publications

Talking Tea with the 3Gs:
The First 10 Years of the Three Generations Book Club (2015)

"Mariage Frères: 150 Years of Tea"
Tea Bits magazine (December 2004)

Website and Links

www.Talking-Tea.com